CHILDREN'S SOCIAL COMPETENCE: THEORY AND INTERVENTION

CHILDREN'S ISSUES, LAWS AND PROGRAMS

Additional books in this series can be found on Nova's website at under the Series tab.

Additional E-books in this series can be found on Nova's website under the E-books tab.

CHILDREN'S ISSUES, LAWS AND PROGRAMS

CHILDREN'S SOCIAL COMPETENCE: THEORY AND INTERVENTION

MELISSA L. GREENE
JO R. HARITON
ANDREW L. ROBINS
AND
BARBARA L. FLYE

Nova Science Publishers, Inc.

New York

NOTICE TO THE READER

The Publisher has taken reasonable care in the preparation of this book, but makes no expressed or implied warranty of any kind and assumes no responsibility for any errors or omissions. No liability is assumed for incidental or consequential damages in connection with or arising out of information contained in this book. The Publisher shall not be liable for any special, consequential, or exemplary damages resulting, in whole or in part, from the readers' use of, or reliance upon, this material.

Independent verification should be sought for any data, advice or recommendations contained in this book. In addition, no responsibility is assumed by the publisher for any injury and/or damage to persons or property arising from any methods, products, instructions, ideas or otherwise contained in this publication.

This publication is designed to provide accurate and authoritative information with regard to the subject matter covered herein. It is sold with the clear understanding that the Publisher is not engaged in rendering legal or any other professional services. If legal or any other expert assistance is required, the services of a competent person should be sought. FROM A DECLARATION OF PARTICIPANTS JOINTLY ADOPTED BY A COMMITTEE OF THE AMERICAN BAR ASSOCIATION AND A COMMITTEE OF PUBLISHERS.

Additional color graphics may be available in the e-book version of this book.

LIBRARY OF CONGRESS CATALOGING-IN-PUBLICATION DATA
Children's social competence : theory and intervention / authors, Melissa L. Greene ... [et al.].
      p. cm.
  Includes index.
  ISBN 978-1-61668-861-5 (softcover)
  1. Social skills in children. 2. Interpersonal relations in children. 3. Children with disabilities. I. Greene, Melissa L.
  BF723.S62C456 2010
  155.4'18--dc22   2010016661

Published by Nova Science Publishers, Inc. † New York

CONTENTS

PREFACE

The current book will discuss peer relationships and social skills in school age children. In the first half of the book, we will review historical and current understanding of the importance of peer relationships and effective social skills for development and well-being. We will review and discuss the concepts of social skills and social competence, as well as current understanding of the social difficulties of children with ADHD, autism spectrum disorders, and Social Anxiety Disorder. We will then present data from an outpatient child psychiatry clinic that describes the diagnoses and social difficulties among school-age children referred for social skills training. The second half of the book will focus on current clinical interventions to assist children with peer relationships. We will review the recent research on the effectiveness of social skills training, and present four commonly utilized training programs. Finally, we will discuss the social skills training program designed and implemented at the Weill Cornell Medical College/New York-Presbyterian Hospital, including the theoretical background, structure and format, as well as interventions to target specific emotional, behavioral, and cognitive skills.

Chapter 1

INTRODUCTION

The significance of peer interactions, relationships, and friendships has a long history in the developmental psychology literature. In the early 20th century, Piaget (1932/1965) discussed the importance of interactions with peers for cognitive and moral development, stressing that it is through interactions with those of equal status (i.e., peers) that essential skills such as interpersonal perspective taking are acquired. Although Piaget did not formally discuss the role of friendships, his theory laid the groundwork for our current understanding of the importance of these relationships for development.

The role of peers in healthy personality development was elaborated upon by Sullivan (1953), and was a significant component of his interpersonal theory. Sullivan proposed that interpersonal needs emerging at each stage of development are met through particular social relationships. According to this theory, peers first come to the fore during what Sullivan called the "juvenile era," when the general peer group provides the necessary need for acceptance. Later, during the pre-adolescent years, the development of a "chumship," a close friendship with a same-sex peer, provides acceptance, validation, and the newly emerging need for intimacy. For Sullivan, these relationships allow the individual to develop the necessary social skills and competencies that contribute to overall healthy development. Although he did not formally test his theory, Sullivan proposed that the absence of friends would lead to poor psychological adjustment, including experiences of loneliness and depression; and specifically, that the absence of a chumship would impact the development of the self and contribute to low self-esteem.

Since Piaget and Sullivan, the developmental functions of peer relationships and friendships have been discussed and elaborated upon by theorists and researchers alike (e.g., Berndt, 1982; Buhrmester, 1996; Buhrmester & Furman, 1987; Hartup, 1996; Ladd, 1999; Newcomb & Bagwell, 1995; 1996; Selman, 1980; Smollar & Youniss, 1982). Owing to increasing understanding of the importance of peers for well-being, a growing body of research has explored peers as a important ecological context of development (Bronfenbrenner, 1979). This work has resulted in an extensive body of research supporting the associations between positive peer relationships and psychological adjustment and well-being (see Kupersmidt & Dodge, 2004 for comprehensive discussion). Early experiences with peers have been repeatedly linked with a range of psychological and psychosocial correlates including internalizing and externalizing behaviors, depression, substance use, loneliness, self-esteem, academic/vocational success, and legal difficulties (e.g., Bukowski *et al.*, 1993; Criss *et al.*, 2002; Erdley *et al.*, 2001; Greene *et al.*, 1999; Greene & Way, 2005; Hoglund *et al.*, 2008; Keefe & Berndt, 1996; Parker & Asher, 1987; Vernberg, 1990; Woodward & Fergusson, 1999). This body of research has explored a variety of constructs including peer acceptance/rejection, friendship/friendlessness, and friendship quality, in an attempt to get a more nuanced understanding of the means by which experiences with peers are related to other aspects of development and well-being.

Furthermore, a large body of both short and long term longitudinal research has established links between experiences with peers during early childhood and psychological adjustment in later childhood, adolescence, and into adulthood (e.g., Bagwell *et al.*, 1998; Coie *et al.*, 1992; Greene *et al.*, 1999; Kupersmidt & Coie, 1990; Ladd & Troop-Gordon, 2003; Ollendick *et al.*, 1992; Parker & Asher, 1987; Woodward & Ferguson, 1999). In general, this research has found strong associations between negative experiences with peers, including peer rejection and/or friendlessness, and later social and emotional maladjustment. For example, in a study spanning a 12 year period, Bagwell and colleagues (1998) examined the unique and combined experiences of the separate predictors of preadolescent dyadic friendship and peer acceptance on adjustment in early adulthood. Their results indicated that experiences of peer rejection during preadolescence were associated with more negative overall adjustment in early adulthood. More specifically, those who had been rejected by peers in fifth grade reported lower school competence, and more trouble with authorities as young adults than their more accepted peers. In addition, in support of Sullivan's (1953) theory of chumships, results indicated that preadolescents who had a close, mutual friendship (i.e., a chum) had more positive self-esteem as young adults than did those who did not have a close friend as a preadolescent.

While early writers posited the "essentialist" theory of peer relationships and friendships (i.e., these experiences are *necessary* for healthy development), there is a bit of a "chicken and egg" question regarding the relationship between early peer experiences and later maladjustment. In other words, what comes first, poor peer relations/peer rejection or maladjustment? Furthermore, are children rejected or friendless because of an underlying problem or disorder that leads to both poor peer relations and poor adjustment? Parker & Asher (1987) provide an excellent overview of the two basic types of models (i.e., causal and incidental), that can be used to explain the relationship between peer relations and adjustment. While there is a significant body of research supporting links between children's behavior and peer acceptance or rejection (e.g., Dodge, 1983; Heiman, 2005), rejected or socially isolated children may also have fewer opportunities to gain the benefits of positive peer experiences, contributing to poorer overall adjustment. Other variables, such as underlying behavioral or emotional disorders, may also contribute to both poor peer interactions and overall maladjustment. Further research is needed to fully understand the complexities of these relationships. In addition, the unique experiences of general peer relations, peer acceptance/rejection, and close friendships may impact development differently (see Newcomb & Bagwell, 1995, Parker & Asher, 1987 for reviews).

Recent advances in our understanding of developmental psychopathology, risk, and resiliency (e.g., Cichetti, 2006) also provide us with models that examine how inherent characteristics of the child (e.g., behavioral inhibition) may interact with the environment (e.g., experiences with peers) to produce developmental outcomes. Advances in statistical modeling, including path analysis, structural equation and multilevel modeling (see Raudenbush & Bryk, 2002; Rogosa & Willett, 1985; Willet & Singer, 2004) are also helping to clarify the complex relationships between these constructs and will allow us to improve our understanding of the potential mechanisms through which peer relationships are related to development and well-being. Greater understanding of these pathways will afford us greater ability to design and tailor appropriate treatment interventions.

Regardless of the explanatory model one adopts, the current literature has made a strong case that that having positive experiences with peers and friends is advantageous for development and well-being. It is now widely accepted that through experiences with peers, children acquire and practice many of the skills that promote effective social relationships (e.g., perspective taking, conflict resolution, cooperation), and that pave the way for the development of healthy relationships later in life. In addition, peers are understood as a vehicle through which children obtain the necessary feelings of acceptance, validation, inclusion, and intimacy that contribute to emotional health and well-being. Finally, in support of Sullivan's (1953) theory, research on the self and self-esteem has consistently supported the importance of peers for healthy development of the "self system" (Berndt & Burgy, 1996; Greene & Way, 2005; Rubin *et al.*, 1995).

However, for a variety of reasons, not all children demonstrate the behaviors that facilitate effective peer interactions, putting them at risk for peer rejection and friendlessness (e.g., Dodge, 1983). Thus, it becomes crucial to identify children for whom peer relationships may be problematic, and to intervene to promote the necessary skills that allow for successful interactions and relationships with peers. When we talk about behaviors that contribute to social interactions and social competence, what we are talking about is the notion of "social skills." Since social skills are the building blocks for our social interactions; and, if one adopts the essentialist perspective, then they are building blocks for healthy development and adjustment.

Chapter 2

SOCIAL SKILLS: DEFINITIONS, CONCEPTUALIZATION ANDCLASSIFICATION

Despite its significance, the term "social skills" appears poorly understood, or at least poorly agreed upon, as a concept in the clinical and research literature. A variety of definitions and conceptualizations of the term has been put forth in the past three decades (see Elliott & Gresham, 1987; Gresham, 1986; Merrell & Gimpel, 1998; Michelson & Mannarino, 1986; Michelson *et al.*, 1983). After reviewing *16* different definitions of social skills that appeared in the literature between 1973 and 1985, and searching for commonalities among them, Merrell and Gimpel defined social skills as: "... learned, composed of specific behaviors, include initiations and responses, maximize social reinforcement, are interactive and situation-specific, and can be specified as targets for intervention" (p. 5).

Gresham (1986) delineated three families of definitions of social skills. First, there are those definitions that rely solely on the presence of *peer acceptance* to define socially skilled behavior. In other words, behaviors that lead to acceptance by one's peer group are deemed socially skilled. As Gresham points out, this definition does not assist us to understand which behaviors are contributing to acceptance or rejection. Thus, from an intervention standpoint, this type of definition is not complete and would not assist in developing appropriate interventions. Next, Gresham distinguishes the *behavioral* definitions of social skills. According to these definitions, socially skilled behaviors are those that maximize reinforcement and minimize punishment. While this definition allows researchers and clinicians to identify specific behaviors, it does not ensure that these behaviors will lead to socially important outcomes, as the mere presence of reinforcement does not ensure social significance. Merrell and Gimpel (1998) note that the majority of definitions they reviewed fall into this category and are popular because they do allow for the specification of behaviors that can be targeted for intervention. Finally, Gresham posits the *social validity* definition of social skills, in which social skills are behaviors that will lead to outcomes deemed valid by the larger society (e.g., peer acceptance). This definition incorporates the advantages of the earlier two, in that behaviors can be specified for intervention, but it is only behaviors that lead to socially valid outcomes that are considered socially skilled.

Thus, the social validity definition allows for a focus on specific behaviors, while emphasizing the importance of a criterion-referenced outcome. In this respect, this definition bears some similarity to the broader notion of "social competence," which is more consistently understood to be a global evaluation of a child's success (or lack thereof) in social interactions. However, important distinctions have been made between these two concepts (Gresham, 1986; Hops & Finch, 1985; McFall, 1982; Merrell & Gimpel, 1998; Spence, 1995). In simplest terms, social skills are those behaviors that can contribute to one's social competence. As such, social competence is the superordinate concept, and contains constructs other than social skills (e.g., motor skills, language skills). A recent model by Spence (2003) underscores the relationship between social skills and competence. This model incorporates both specific skills (e.g., interpersonal problem solving skills, social cognitive skills), as well as environmental variables, such as opportunities to learn behaviors through modeling, and contingencies found in the environment. Thus, it is the interplay of the child's skills, and the important developmental contexts (e.g., family, peers, school) that contribute to social responding and social competence.

As clinicians working directly with children and their families, both concepts, social skills and social competence, are extremely useful, as is the distinction between them. For the purpose of the current discussion, as well as our larger clinical work, we adopt the notion that social skills are the specific behaviors that will contribute to an individual's broader social competence. Thus, in our assessment and understanding of a child's social difficulties, we must take into account the presence or absence of specific skills, the social validity of these skills, environmental variables, and social competence as evaluated by parents, teachers, and the child himself.

CLASSIFYING SOCIAL SKILLS
AND SOCIAL SKILLS DEFICITS

Given that the concept of social skills is difficult to agree upon, it is not surprising that there are multiple classifications systems that have been presented in the literature. A general, but extremely useful model is that of Gresham and colleagues (see Elliott & Gresham, 1987; Gresham, 1986 for discussions). Drawn from social learning theory (Bandura, 1977), Gresham presents a two-way classification scheme based on the absence or presence in specific skills (i.e., a *skills* deficit or a *performance* deficit), and the presence or absence of emotional arousal (e.g., anxiety). Thus, children's social skills difficulties can be classified in one of four categories. When emotional arousal is absent, social difficulties are classified as either *social skills deficits*, which occur when a child does not have knowledge of how to perform specific social behaviors; or as *social performance deficits*, when children have appropriate knowledge of skills, but do not perform them at a level that leads to social competence. When emotional arousal is present, and has impeded the acquisition of social skills, this is a *self-control social skill deficit*; when emotional arousal is present, and impairs a child's ability to perform skills, this would be classified as a *self-control performance deficit*. For example, children on the autism spectrum are commonly conceptualized as lacking the social know how to be effective socially (i.e., having *skills* deficits), while children with ADHD, or with other externalizing behavior disorders are believed to have the skills yet lack the ability to perform them consistently (i.e., *performance* deficits). However, as will be discussed later in this book, individual children, as well as children within diagnostic categories may have both skills and performance deficits, rendering a comprehensive evaluation and assessment of social functioning essential for appropriate treatment planning.

While children may have some combination of skills and performance deficits, we have also found it useful in our clinical work to classify social skills more specifically. We observe that children who experience difficulties with social interactions and relationships have problems in the ways that they feel, act, and think in social situations. As a result, we have found that conceptualizing children's specific skills in terms of affective or emotional, behavioral and cognitive domains has been a useful tool in our clinical work. These three broad domains of functioning can be broken further down into sub-domains, with skills subsumed under each of these. For example, areas that fall under affective or emotional functioning would include emotion regulation, emotional empathy, and self-esteem, and would incorporate specific skills such as anger management, and emotional reactivity. Behavioral domains would include communication skills (both verbal and non-verbal), prosocial behaviors, and play skills. Cognitive domains would include social information processing, theory of mind, and effort control. A more comprehensive list of domains and skills can be seen in Table 1. It is important to note that this list is not exhaustive, and certain skills (e.g., impulse control) are found under more than one domain. As clinicians working with children who present a variety of social difficulties, this classification scheme has appeal and can assist in the design and matching of interventions to more effectively target and improve children's social difficulties.

Table 1. Emotional, Behavioral, and Cognitive Domains of Social Skills

Domain	Sub-Domains	Skills
Emotional	Emotion Regulation	Recognition/coping with feelings; emotional expression; impulse control; frustration tolerance
	Empathy	Identification of others' feeling states
	Self-esteem	Realistic self-esteem, feelings about self
Behavioral	Communication Skills	Non-verbal/pragmatics: Eye contact, facial expressions, body language. Verbal: Initiating conversation, responding, verbal turn taking, verbal self-control, compliments, greetings/goodbyes, use of humor
	Play/Task Behaviors	Sharing, turn taking, on-task behavior, task completion, cooperation,/compromise, conflict resolution, sportsmanship
	Prosocial Behaviors	Assertion, self-control, social initiation, following rules/directions, conflict resolution, giving/receiving feedback, compromise, cooperation, flexibility
Cognitive	Social Information Processing	Attribution of intent/motives, interpersonal perspective taking, emotion recognition, reading/understanding social cues, theory of mind
	Problem Solving	Social problem solving, means end -thinking, generating alternative solutions
	Effortful Control	Impulse control, response inhibition, attention/concentration, on-task/on-topic behavior
	Cognitive Flexibility	Making transitions, set-shifting, generating alternatives
	Social Knowledge	Knowledge of appropriate social behavior; understanding of friendships and relationships
	Self-awareness	Self-monitoring, reflective-function, self-evaluation

Chapter 3

SOCIAL SKILLS DEFICITS AMONG CLINICAL POPULATIONS

Children seeking evaluation and treatment for social difficulties present a variety of emotional and behavioral disorders. Many of these children are described by their parents as "struggling socially." Parents report poor social competence, and describe their children as having difficulty engaging in the give and take of social interactions and consequently, having few friends and limited social activities and experiences. Research confirms these parental reports. Children in therapy are twice as likely to have peer problems when compared with children who are not in therapy (Frankel & Feinberg, 2002; Malik & Furman, 1993; Thorell & Rydell, 2008). Despite what clinicians know to be true of children in psychiatric treatment, it is interesting to note that, with the exception of the autism spectrum diagnoses (e.g., Autistic Disorder, Asperger's Disorder, and Pervasive Developmental Disorder Not Otherwise Specified), social skills deficits and poor social competence are not included as core symptoms in the current diagnostic nomenclature (DSM-IV-TR; American Psychiatric Association, 2000). Thus, despite our understanding of the importance of peer relationships and friendships for adjustment and well-being, social difficulties are often relegated to the back seat in treatment.

In the following sections, we will present an overview of some of the more common social difficulties found among school-age children with autism spectrum disorders, Attention Deficit Hyperactivity Disorder, and anxiety disorders, specifically Social Anxiety Disorder or Social Phobia. Diagnostically different groups of children tend to have different types of social difficulties, but there is a high incidence of comorbidity, as well as a great variety of presentations among children within each diagnostic category.

Furthermore, variables such as age, gender, intellectual or cognitive abilities, and developmental level also play a role in the presentation of social skills and social competence, further complicating the picture. Finally, while this list of diagnoses is certainly not exhaustive, and children with other psychiatric diagnoses often experience social difficulties as well; we have chosen to highlight these three diagnoses because they constitute the majority of diagnoses that we see in our clinical work with children for social skills training in an outpatient child psychiatry clinic.

AUTISM SPECTRUM DISORDERS

Qualitative impairment in social interaction is a fundamental aspect of an autism spectrum diagnosis, according to the current *Diagnostic and Statistical Manual of Mental Disorders* (DSM-IV-TR; American Psychiatric Association, 2000). Thus, children with diagnoses of Autism, Asperger's Disorder, or Pervasive Developmental Disorder, Not Otherwise Specified (PDD, NOS) face significant social challenges. These children are generally described as lacking social understanding, having deficient social skills, and engaging socially much less often than their typical peers (Kasari & Rotheram-Fuller, 2007). When they do interact with peers, deficits in empathy, expression of emotion, appreciation of social cues, understanding of how to play with others, and interest in participating in group or team activities contribute to impaired social reciprocity (Attwood, 2007). Contrary to clinical lore, many authors report that children on the autism spectrum show a desire for interpersonal interactions and friendships, and that comorbid anxiety and depression often develop as a result of their inability to establish friendships (Attwood, 2007; Kasari & Rotheram-Fuller, 2007; Myles & Southwick, 1999). The specific social skills that bear on these functional deficits can be categorized into affective or emotional, behavioral, and cognitive domains.

Difficulties in the emotional domain that impact social competence include limited empathic ability and difficulty understanding and expressing emotions (Attwood, 2007). Children on the autism spectrum are often perceived as emotionally blunted, with flat affect and flat tone of voice, and they lack precision and subtlety in their expression of emotions. In contrast to their typical, flat presentation, these children also have significant difficulties with affect regulation. They can become easily agitated, overwhelmed, or overly excited, especially in highly stimulating, unpredictable, or unstructured situations (Myles & Southwick, 1999). Rage reactions and temper outbursts are not uncommon when these children experience stress or frustration (Myles & Southwick, 1999; Powers & Poland, 2003). Reports of emotional exhaustion are also common (Attwood, 2007) as a result of the amount of mental effort required for a child with an autism spectrum disorder to process social information throughout the day. Additionally, social anxiety often accompanies autism spectrum disorders (Attwood, 2007; Myles & Southwick, 1999). Some families report that their child has seemed "hard wired" for anxious reactions, including panic attacks, since birth. Other children on the autism spectrum develop anxiety in social interactions because these situations can be fast paced, unpredictable, and ambiguous, or because of a history of unsuccessful interactions or victimization/bullying. Low self-esteem and low self-confidence can also develop as a result of challenges and failures in socializing (Attwood, 2007; Myles & Southwick, 1999). It is noteworthy that the combination of emotional exhaustion, anxiety, social failure, and low self-esteem can lead to clinical depression.

Children on the autism spectrum display specific behaviors that inhibit social success. Teachers and parents indicate that primary school-age children diagnosed with autism spectrum disorders show deficits in the social behaviors of cooperation, assertion, and self-control across a variety of real-life settings relative to their typically developing peers (Macintosh & Dissanayake, 2006; Murray et al., 2009). Social communication is affected by deficits in non-verbal communication such as limited facial expressions, peculiar stiff gaze, limited use of gestures, and clumsy body language (Attwood, 2007), while verbal communication can be pedantic and self-focused, and include deficits such as little or no speech prosody and flat tone of voice (Gunter et al., 2002). These children make fewer attempts to engage peers in interaction (Kasari & Rotheram-Fuller, 2007), and when they do interact, they are prone to act in unusual ways or make inappropriate comments because they are not aware of social rules or the effect of their behavior on others (Myles & Southwick, 1999). As a result, they can be perceived as rude or insensitive.

In conjunction with these emotional and behavioral difficulties, children with autism spectrum diagnoses also struggle with core cognitive functions. Their cognitive styles are characterized by narrowly defined interests; rigid, literal, and concrete thinking; distractibility and inattention; difficulties with problem solving and organizational skills; and difficulty discerning relevant from irrelevant stimuli (Myles & Southwick, 1999). Children on the autism spectrum have poor theory of mind abilities; that is to say, they struggle with understanding the beliefs and emotions of others. They tend to have difficulty taking another person's perspective, attending to and reading social cues, and understanding verbal and nonverbal communication (Kasari & Rotheram-Fuller, 2007). They tend to be rule bound but ironically, do not understand or appreciate the rules of social interaction (Attwood, 2007). Furthermore, although their intellectual abilities may be advanced or "adult-like," as described by Myles & Southwick (1999), this may also impact their ability to relate comfortably with same-age peers.

There is significant overlap between the cognitive profiles of children with autism spectrum disorders, particularly Asperger's Disorder, and Nonverbal Learning Disorder (NVLD) (Gunter *et al.*, 2002; Rourke, 1989 & 1995; Volkmar & Klin, 1998). Children with Asperger's Disorder often have an NVLD cognitive profile, while some children with NVLD do not meet criteria for an autism spectrum diagnosis (Volkmar & Klin, 1998). As such, it can be helpful to understand the cognitive deficits associated with NVLD, as this can yield a greater appreciation of the way children with autism spectrum disorders perceive the world.

Rourke (1989, 1995) and others have described the neuropsychological characteristics of NVLD as including deficits in visual-spatial organizational abilities. For example, these children may stand too close or too far from others, or fail to appreciate subtle visual details and body language in nonverbal communication (Thompson, 1997). They may have deficits in nonverbal problem-solving, concept formation, and hypothesis testing, and have difficulty understanding cause and effect relationships (Rourke, 1989). As such, they typically do not benefit from informational feedback in novel situations. Additionally, children with NVLD have extreme difficulty adapting to novel and complex situations. They overly rely on rote, previously learned, or overused strategies and rubrics (Rourke, 1989). Cognitively, they tend to be rigid, concrete, all-or-none thinkers. They demonstrate strong memory skills for facts and details but have difficulty making inferences, seeing the "big picture," and integrating and synthesizing information (Thomson, 1997). This difficulty is particularly challenging in the social arena, where one must constantly integrate multisensory information like nonverbal social cues and verbal content in conversations while simultaneously accounting for factors like context and gestalt. These children also have deficits in executive functioning, such as planning, organizing, set shifting, generating alternatives, initiating, and executing (Rourke, 1989); leading to problems with self-advocacy, social planning, social problem-solving, and follow-through. Thus, children with this cognitive profile, regardless of a formal diagnosis of an autism spectrum disorder, will have significant difficulties understanding and managing the complex, ambiguous, nonverbal, and unpredictable social world.

The interplay often associated with the specific emotional, behavioral, and cognitive deficits has a clear and fundamental impact on the social interactions of children on the autism spectrum. Impaired social functioning, results from deficits in social skills, in turn leads to social discomfort, awkwardness, confusion, and rejection, leaving these children feeling lonely, discouraged, socially anxious, socially incompetent, and potentially depressed into adolescence and beyond. This common pattern of skills deficits suggests specific targets of intervention (Volkmar & Klin, 1998), and the common experience of social isolation make this clinical population particularly well suited for group interventions.

ATTENTION DEFICIT HYPERACTIVITY DISORDER

In contrast to autism spectrum diagnoses, a social skills deficit or impairment in social interaction is not required or even included as a core feature for diagnosing ADHD (DSM-IV-TR; APA, 2000). However, children with ADHD are frequently impaired in multiple areas of life, including peer relationships (see Barkley, 2003). In support of clinical observations and parental concerns, a large body of research describes impairment in the peer relations of children with ADHD (e.g., Abikoff et al., 2004; Barkley et al., 1990; Biederman, 2005; Erhardt & Hinshaw, 1994; Frankel & Feinberg, 2002; Guevremont, 1990; Guevremont & Dumas, 1994; Greene et al., 1999; Hinshaw, 1994; Hinshaw & Melnick, 1995; Hoza et al., 2005; Maedgen & Carlson, 2000; Nijmeijer et al., 2008; Pope et al., 1989; Thorell & Rydell, 2008). This body of research demonstrates that children with ADHD more often experience peer rejection or neglect, are less socially preferred, have fewer dyadic friendships, and more often affiliate with deviant peers. These social difficulties may persist into adolescence, even in the absence of continued ADHD symptoms (Bagwell et al., 2001).

A variety of mechanisms have been suggested through which the core deficits of the disorder may negatively impact peer interactions and relationships. For example, difficulties with emotional regulation have been discussed as a central feature of ADHD (Barkley, 1997). Children with ADHD may have intense emotional reactions, quick displays of temper, "mood swings" and poor frustration tolerance. These "emotional difficulties" may contribute to maladaptive social behaviors including social withdrawal, disruptive and aggressive behavior, and poor interpersonal problem solving (Barkley, 1997; Eisenberg et al., 1994; Erhardt & Hinshaw, 1994;

Guevremont & Dumas, 1994; Hinshaw & Melnick, 1994; Landau & Milich, 1988; Maedgen & Carlson, 2000; Melnick & Hinshaw, 1996).

While current diagnostic criteria do not mandate social difficulties as a requirement for making the diagnosis of ADHD, a quick look at the criteria, includes items such as "often does not seem to listen when spoken to," "often talks excessively," and "often interrupts or intrudes on others" (DSM-IV-TR; APA, 2000, p. 92), makes it no surprise that the behaviors of these children interfere with their social functioning. Typically, children with ADHD seek social contact, but are often observed to be intrusive or inappropriate (e.g., Frankel & Fienberg, 2002; Erhardt & Hinshaw, 1994; Wheeler & Carlson, 1994). When interacting with peers, children with ADHD demonstrate more negative behaviors, including hostility and aggression, than other children (e.g., Buhrmester et al., 1992; Hinshaw & Melnick, 1995; Thurber et al., 2002). In addition, their behaviors are often not appropriate or are disruptive for the situation (e.g., running around, interrupting or talking over peers) (e.g., Barkley, 1997; Guevremont, 1990; Landau & Moore, 1991). Due to impulsivity and difficulties with attention, children with ADHD may have poor social communication skills, frequently changing topics, interrupting peers, and/or giving inappropriate responses. In general, these children seem to have difficulty with the give-and-take required for effective communication (e.g., Landau & Milich, 1988; Guevremont & Dumas, 1994). Thus, given these disruptive, aggressive and/or inattentive behaviors, it is no surprise that children with ADHD are more frequently rejected by peers, achieve low social status, and often fail to develop a best friend.

The presence of comorbid aggression and/or conduct disorder seems to exacerbate the social difficulties of these children (Gresham et al., 1998; Guevremont & Dumas, 1994; Jensen et al., 2001; Melnick & Hinshaw, 2000). This is significant given the high degree of comorbidity between ADHD and aggression or conduct problems, with estimates ranging from 30 to 50 percent (Barkley, 2003; Biederman, 2005; Hinshaw, 1987; Spencer, 2006). A recent study of children with ADHD attempted to tease apart the direct effects of the core symptoms (e.g., impulsivity, hyperactivity and inattention), from the effects of aggressive behavior, on social functioning (Diamantopoulou et al., 2005). Results revealed that ADHD symptoms were directly related to children's low social preference, but did not account for it exclusively. Children's low levels of prosocial behavior, and more frequent aggressive behavior and internalizing problems were also strongly related to experiences of peer dislike, rejected peer status, and poor peer relations. The presence of co-morbid aggression among children with ADHD has also been linked to poorer social functioning later in life (Bagwell *et al.*, 2001).

Difficulties with social cognition, or the processing of social information, also seem to contribute to the problematic social behaviors and relationships of children with ADHD. The core features of the disorder, including inattention and impulsivity, may make children with ADHD prone to gather less information, less attentive to relevant social cues, and more likely to make misattributions regarding the intent and meaning of other's behavior (Coy *et al.*, 2001; Guevremont & Dumas, 1994). In addition, research demonstrates that early experience of peer rejection, a frequent occurrence for children with ADHD, may modify how these children attend to and process social information (Dodge *et al.*, 1990; Dodge *et al.*, 2003). As a result of these social cognitive biases, children with ADHD are more likely to react in social situations with negative emotions and/or aggressive behavior (e.g., Crick & Dodge, 1996; Dodge, 1983; Milich & Dodge, 1984; Thurber *et al.*, 2002). Over time, these hostile attribution biases may get confirmed, as these children elicit true negative responses from peers. Thus, a maladaptive cycle develops, contributing to poorer social functioning.

Children with ADHD and those at risk for ADHD also have impairments in their ability to recognize the emotions of themselves and others, further complicating their processing of social information (Katz-Gold *et al.*, 2007; Katz-Gold & Priel, 2009; Quiggle *et al.*, 1992). Research also demonstrates that these children are frequently inaccurate in their self-perceptions in social situations, often overestimating their competence (e.g., Hoza *et al.*, 2002; 2004). Taken together, the social-cognitive deficits may contribute to a host of social difficulties, including misunderstandings and conflict with peers, aggressive behavior, and experiences of rejection and isolation.

Difficulties with inattention may also contribute uniquely to poor social relationships, independent of aggressive or disruptive behavior (Pope *et al.*, 1991). Indeed, it has been proposed that children with the predominantly inattentive subtype of ADHD may have a different profile of social skills deficits compared with their more hyperactive peers (Barkley, 1997; Maedgen & Carlson, 2000; Wheeler & Carlson, 1994). Wheeler and Carlson (1994) have suggested that children with the predominantly inattentive subtype of ADHD may have greater deficits in social understanding and knowledge (skills deficits, according to Gresham's classification), and fewer difficulties in social performance, as compared to their hyperactive peers. Recent research examining social deficits in children with ADHD-Combined and ADHD-Inattentive subtypes has confirmed distinct profiles of social difficulties for children with these two subtypes (Maedgen & Carlson, 2000). In this study, children with ADHD-Combined showed greater difficulties with aggressive behavior and emotion regulation (e.g., more intense emotional reactions), while children with ADHD-Inattentive type were characterized by greater passivity in social interactions and a lack of social knowledge.

Children with ADHD may also have different ideas and expectations of peer relationships and friendships, which may further complicate their social difficulties. For example, a recent study of ADHD children found differences in the definition of a "best friend" (Heiman, 2005). In this study, children with ADHD were more likely to define a "best friend" as more of a companion for fun and mutual entertainment, while their peers identified a best friend as someone who provides emotional support and acts as a partner to share thoughts and secrets. This research suggests that children with ADHD have different ideas and expectations of peer relationships and friendships than their typical peers. Differences in expectations and understanding of what makes a friend or a best friend may hinder the formation of dyadic friendships for children with ADHD.

Thus, the social picture for children with ADHD is complicated by a variety of difficulties and deficits in the emotional, behavioral, and cognitive realms. This picture is further complicated by the varying presentations of children with ADHD, including both the inattentive and hyperactive/combined subtypes of the disorder, as well as the presence of comorbid aggression or conduct problems. A comprehensive evaluation of the specific social deficits will be necessary in order to design treatment interventions, including group treatment, to target the skills of children with ADHD and other behavioral disorders. Given that these children seem to struggle in both their skills, knowledge, and perceptions of social behavior and relationships, as well as in their broader cognitive and emotional functioning, a thorough assessment and multimodal treatment seems warranted.

SOCIAL ANXIETY DISORDER

Children with anxiety disorders, specifically Social Anxiety Disorder or Social Phobia, are often found to have co-occurring social problems, including peer rejection, fewer friends/poorer friendship quality, and increased peer victimization (Beidel & Turner, 1998; Beidel et al., 1999; Bernstein et al., 2008; Erath et al., 2007; Greco & Morris, 2005; La Greca & Lopez, 1998; Spence et al., 1999). In children, the diagnosis of Social Anxiety Disorder requires the presence of severe anxiety in interactions with peers and/or avoidance of these interactions (DSM-IV-TR; APA, 2000). Children with social anxiety may present with a combination of performance deficits, as well as skills deficits. For example, severe anxiety in social situations may interfere with these children's ability to display appropriate, prosocial behaviors, leading to peer rejection, social withdrawal and avoidance. Furthermore, as a result of their tendency to avoid anxiety-provoking peer interactions and/or to be neglected by peers, children with social anxiety may also have limited ability to develop and practice age-appropriate social skills, further contributing to poor social outcomes (Greco & Morris, 2005; Rubin & Burgess, 2001).

Social anxiety has been repeatedly linked with measures and ratings of objective social behaviors (Beidel et al., 1999; Bernstein et al., 2008; Greco & Morris, 2005; Rao et al., 2007), with socially anxious or phobic children and adolescents often rated as less socially skilled by parents, teachers, and clinicians compared with their peers. Deficits that have been noted in the research and clinical literature include lower levels of social initiation and interaction (e.g., Beidel et al., 1999; Spence et al., 1999); shorter responses (e.g., Morgan & Banerjee, 2006; Spence et al., 1999) and longer speech latencies (Beidel et al., 1999); fewer prosocial behaviors (e.g., Erath et al., 2007); and greater difficulty recognizing facial expressions (e.g., Simonian et al., 2001). Due to anxiety brought on by social interactions, these children also engage in more avoidant behaviors than their peers (Beidel et al., 1999).

Cognitive difficulties, particularly the processing of social information, may also contribute to the peer-related difficulties experienced by anxious children. Interestingly, a growing body of research suggests that children with social anxiety do not necessarily have either behavioral skills deficits or objectively rated social performance deficits (Cartwright-Hatton et al., 2003; 2005), but suffer from difficulties in their perceptions of social situations. In these recent studies, children with social anxiety were rated as equally socially skilled as their peers on social behaviors (e.g., smiling, eye contact, speech). However, these children, when asked to rate their own performance, rate themselves as less socially competent. Thus, this research suggests that social difficulties of anxious children may be due in part to negative self-appraisals of their social behavior. These children also anticipate that they will perform poorly in social situations (Morgan & Banerjee, 2006), and anticipate negative consequences to result from social interactions (Erath et al., 2007; Morgan & Banerjee, 2006). Thus, similar to the difficulties observed for children with

ADHD, these results illustrate how social-information processing and cognitive biases may affect behavioral performance (Crick & Dodge, 1994).

Taken together, the literature suggests that children with social anxiety may present with a variety of emotional, behavioral, and cognitive difficulties that contribute to problems with peer relationships. Furthermore, the mechanisms that contribute to these children's social difficulties are varied and complex, including both performance (e.g., due to inhibitory anxiety) and skills deficits, and their interactions. A thorough and comprehensive assessment of social behaviors and skills, and thoughtful treatment planning that can target emotional, behavioral, and cognitive factors, is necessary to design effective interventions to improve these children's social competence.

Chapter 4

A STUDY OF CHILDREN REFERRED FOR OUTPATIENT SOCIAL SKILLS TRAINING

Given the variety of social difficulties and deficits among children with psychiatric disorders, two of the authors (MLG and JRH) were involved in a study conducted in an outpatient child and adolescent psychiatry clinic. Their goal was to examine more closely the children who are referred to the clinic for social skills training. We had the following questions in mind when we began this investigation: 1.What primary psychiatric diagnoses referred children for social skills training? 2. How do children referred for social skills training perceive their peer relationships and friendships? 3. In what domains of social functioning do these children have difficulty? 4. Finally, do children referred for social skills training struggle in other areas of emotional and behavioral functioning, and is functioning with peers related to other aspects of emotional and behavioral functioning? We hoped that by addressing these questions through a systematic investigation, we could better tailor our group treatment and interventions to meet the needs of our clients. As this was an exploratory study, we did not have any a priori hypotheses and hoped simply to describe and characterize the children that we are serving.

PARTICIPANTS

Participants in the current study were 36 children enrolled in our social skills group training program, as well as their parents. Children ranged in age from 6.5 years through 12 years (mean of 9.4 years). On average, children had attended 13.22 group sessions upon entry into the study (this ranged from children who had not attended any group session to one child who had already attended 78 group sessions). These children were 69% male and of various ethnicities (55% Caucasian, 8% African American, 14% Hispanic, 3% Asian American, and 11% mixed or other). The majority (64%) of these children were receiving special education services.

We also interviewed 30 children from the community to serve as our control group. These children could not be receiving any psychiatric services from mental health or medical professionals. While our control group was of similar age as our referred children (mean of 9.0 years), there were important differences between the groups. The control group was more female (63%), less ethnically diverse (77% of children were Caucasian), and less likely to be receiving special education services (10%).

MEASURES

Because we were interested in both children's perceptions of their peer relationships and their parent's more objective report on social skills and/or social competence, we used a multi-informant method. A chart review was also conducted in order to collect information regarding diagnosis and treatment. Children were interviewed using the Cornell Interview of Children's Perceptions of Friendships and Peer Relations (Kernberg et al., 1992), a semi-structured interview assessing children's perceptions of their functioning with peers and friends. The interview consists of 87 items that are scored dichotomously. It yields a total score, with higher scores representing poorer perceived friendship quality. It has shown to discriminate between clinical and non-clinical populations (Kernberg et al., 1992), and we found it to have good internal consistency ($\alpha = .79$). In order to assess parent-rated social skills, they were asked to compete the parent form of the Social Skills Rating Form (SSRS; Gresham & Elliott, 1990), which contains 55 items assessing overall social skills on five subscales (assertion, cooperation, self-control, responsibility and problem behaviors). Two of the subscales, Assertion (e.g., "Initiates conversations with peers") and Self-Control (e.g., "Controls temper in conflict situations with peers") tap into peer relationships and were the focus of our interest. This measure has been used widely (e.g., Epp, 2008; Greco & Morris, 2005) and its authors have reported strong psychometric properties (Gresham & Elliott, 1990).

In order to examine the relationships between peer relations and friendships and other indices of social and emotional functioning, we asked parents to complete the Child Behavior Checklist (CBCL; Achenbach, 1991), a 131 item measure of internalizing and externalizing symptoms. For the purpose of the current analyses, we utilized the t-scores for the total internalizing and externalizing subscales. This measure has also been used widely in clinical and research settings (e.g., Thurber *et al.*, 2002) and has shown good psychometric properties (Achenbach & Rescorla, 2004). Children completed the Self-Perception Profile for Children (SPPC; Harter, 1985), a 36 item measure of self-esteem in five domains (social acceptance, athletic competence, scholastic competence, behavioral conduct, and physical appearance), plus global self-esteem. This measure has also been used extensively in research (e.g., Hoza *et al.*, 2004), and has demonstrated good psychometric properties (Harter, 1999).

PROCEDURE

Referred children were recruited from a roster of children currently enrolled in our social skills training program. They were contacted by a member of the research team who provided them with a brief description of the study. Children and parents who agreed to participate were scheduled to come in and meet with one of our interviewers at a later time. Children in the control group were recruited from flyers and ads in the local community. For children in both groups, written consent was obtained from parents, and verbal assent was obtained from the children. While children completed the interview, parents were asked to complete the study questionnaires. The entire session took approximately one hour and children were given a choice of movie passes or a gift certificate to a local book store in exchange for participation.

RESULTS

To address our first research question, descriptive statistics were used to examine the diagnostic make up of children enrolled in our social skills program. Our results revealed that our population is heterogeneous with regard to diagnosis. Forty percent of our children had a primary diagnosis of

Attention Deficit Hyperactivity Disorder (primarily ADHD-Combined type), while 24% had a primary diagnosis of a autism spectrum disorder (either Asperger's Disorder or Pervasive Developmental Disorder, Not Otherwise Specified). Sixteen percent had an Adjustment Disorder, and twenty percent were classified as "other" (anxiety or mood disorder). Forty-seven percent had more than one psychiatric diagnosis, and 50 percent were receiving additional services (e.g., medication management or individual psychotherapy).

Our second and third research questions addressed children's perceptions of their peer relationships and friendships, and parent-reported social skills. To answer these questions, we used independent samples t-tests to compare referred children and their peers on scores from the Cornell Interview and the SSRS. Overall, results of the interview reveal that referred children perceive their peer relationships and friendships as significantly poorer than children in the control group. In order to get a more nuanced picture of these children's perceptions of their friendships, we examined how children endorsed specific items on the interview. While referred and control children did not differ significantly in their report of having friends and having a best friend, children referred for social skills training were more likely to report feeling "not liked by peers" ($\chi^2(1) = 7.82, p < .01$), and a trend towards significance revealed that children referred for social skills training were more likely to report wishing they had more friends, as compared with children in the control group ($\chi^2(1) = 3.09, p < .10$). Parents also reported that children in the social skills training program showed poorer skills with peers in both the areas of cooperation and assertion. Means, standard deviations, and t-scores for these variables can be seen in Table 2.

Our fourth research question addressed whether children referred for social skills training struggle in other areas of emotional and behavioral functioning. We used independent samples t-tests to examine differences between referred and control children on parent reported internalizing and externalizing symptoms, and child reported self-esteem. Our results revealed that children in our social skills training program report significantly poorer self-esteem in all domains, and parents report more internalizing and externalizing problems. Means, standard deviations, and t-scores for these variables can be seen in Table 2. Bivariate correlations for the total sample were used to examine the relationships between children's perceptions of their social skills, parent-rated social skills, internalizing and externalizing symptoms, and self-esteem. These correlations can be seen in Table 3. Significant positive associations were found between children's perceptions of their peer relationships and all domains of self-esteem. Children's perceptions of their peer relations were negatively associated with parent-reported internalizing and externalizing problems. Parent reports of children's skills in the areas of assertion and cooperation were also strongly, negatively related to both internalizing and externalizing problems, and parent-reported assertion was significantly correlated with children's self-esteem (although parent reported cooperation was not related to self-esteem).

**Table 2. Means, standard deviations, and t-scores
for child and parent reported variables as a function of group
(social skills training and control)**

| Variable | Group | | | | |
| | SST | | Control | | |
	M	SD	M	SD	T
Peer Relations/ Friendships	106.00	6.82	98.27	6.62	4.65***
SSRS: Assertion	10.65	2.99	16.72	2.64	-8.26***
SSRS: Self-Control	10.60	3.39	14.28	3.35	-4.19***
Internalizing Problems	61.20	12.57	45.24	9.18	5.69***
Externalizing Problems	55.94	14.27	43.66	8.20	4.31***
Global Self-Esteem	18.89	5.64	21.53	3.30	-2.19*
Social Acceptance	14.81	5.31	19.53	3.83	-3.88***
Athletic Competence	14.70	4.75	18.67	4.05	-3.40**
Scholastic Competence	17.48	5.23	20.00	3.70	-2.12*
Behavioral Conduct	16.81	6.03	21.37	3.49	-3.53**
Physical Appearance	17.37	5.64	21.83	2.97	-3.79***

Note. $* p < .05, ** p < .01, *** p < .001$.

DISCUSSION

Our exploratory study found that children referred for social skills training are heterogeneous with regard to diagnosis. Similar to what has been reported in meta-analyses of group therapy programs for children (Hoag & Burlingame, 1997), a large percentage of children referred for social skills training have a diagnosis of ADHD. Autism spectrum diagnoses were also strongly represented, and there was substantial diagnostic comorbidity. Nearly fifty percent of children in our sample carried more than one diagnosis.

Table 3. Bivariate correlations between study variables

		2	3	4	5	6	7	8	9	10	11
1	Peer Relations/ Friendships	-.39**	-.45***	.34**	.36**	-.48***	-.57***	-.45***	-.55***	-.68***	-.51***
2	SSRS: Assertion	--	.63***	-.55***	-.47***	.32*	.39**	.47***	.34*	.41**	.35**
3	SSRS: Self-Control	--	--	-.60***	-.68***	.18	.09	.15	.07	.22	.25+
4	Internalizing Problems	--	--	--	.74***	-.27*	-.15	-.28*	-.27+	-.33*	-.24+
5	Externalizing Problems	--	--	--	--	-.27*	-.22	-.12	-.23+	-.34*	-.28*
6	Global Self-Esteem	--	--	--	--	--	.64***	.57***	.67***	.69***	.74***
7	Social Acceptance	--	--	--	--	--	--	.57***	.57***	.70***	.71***
8	Athletic Competence	--	--	--	--	--	--	--	.56***	.59***	.54***
9	Scholastic Competence	--	--	--	--	--	--	--	--	.66***	.57***
10	Behavioral Conduct	--	--	--	--	--	--	--	--	--	.74***
11	Physical Appearance	--	--	--	--	--	--	--	--	--	--

Note. + $p < .10$; * $p < .05$, ** $p < .01$; *** $p < .001$.

Thus, our clinic, and others like it are providing social skills training to a population with a variety of difficulties. Although we examined any possible differences in parent reported social skills and children's perceptions of peer relations between children with autism spectrum diagnoses and the children with Attention Deficit Hyperactivity Disorder, we were not able to detect any significant differences. This may be due to our relatively small sample, and therefore limited statistical power, but also may be in part due to comorbidity and overlap in social difficulties among groups. As our population consists of children with autism spectrum disorders, attention deficit disorders, as well as mood and anxiety disorders; our social skills training program needs to address the social difficulties of a diagnostically varied group.

We found that both children and parents reported impaired social skills and peer relationships. Children referred for social skills training were more likely to feel disliked by peers and to wish for more friends. Parents reported that these children have difficulties in peer related domains of Assertion and Self-control. These children also reported impaired self-esteem, both globally and in specific domains, and parents reported greater internalizing and externalizing symptoms. These results reinforce our comprehensive focus on the development and promotion of skills in the emotional, behavioral and cognitive domains. It also suggests that children who are referred for social skills training may need additional services as well, and a comprehensive evaluation should be a part of any social skills training program.

Chapter 5

SOCIAL SKILLS TRAINING:
RESEARCH AND CLINICAL METHODS

During the mid 70's and early 80's, when the literature began to surface on the negative effects of poor peer relationships, social skills training interventions began to proliferate in schools and clinics. Traditional methods incorporated into social skills training programs include modeling, operant conditioning, coaching and direct instruction, as well as opportunities for practicing skills (See Merrell & Gimpel, 1998; Michelson *et al.*, 1983 for discussions).These interventions allow children to develop skills they do not have, and also enhance skills that they may not be able to perform effectively.

There is a wealth of literature examining the effectiveness of social skills training interventions for children in a variety of settings (e.g., schools, clinics) and with a range of clinical and non-clinical presentations. Due to the extensive number of interventions and studies, and their frequent small sample sizes and limited statistical power, this research has often been examined through meta-analyses (see Maag, 2006 for a recent review of reviews). Recent meta-analyses have found overall effect sizes for social skills training to range from small (e.g., Bellini *et al.*, 2007; Quinn *et al.*, 1999) to moderate (Beelman *et al.*, 1994; Schneider, 1992; Schneider & Byrne, 1985). When examining this body of research, authors almost uniformly note that, despite what appears to be an abundance of research attempting to examine the effects of social skills training on children's development and well being, it is difficult to draw many firm conclusions (e.g., Maag, 2006). This is due in part to methodological differences in the definition of social skills or social competence, the implementation of social skills training, and the manner in which assessments and evaluations are conducted (Maag, 2006; Rao *et al.*, 2008).

With these limitations in mind, what follows is a brief review of some of the recent research examining social skills training with clinical and non-clinical populations and some tentative conclusions that could inform clinical practice and research. While the focus of this discussion and our clinical work is with social skills training in outpatient settings, studies drawn from school and other non-clinical settings can also provide useful information. We will then present a brief overview of four commonly utilized social skills training programs, and describe the program that we have developed at Weill Cornell Medical College/New York Presbyterian Hospital.

SOCIAL SKILLS TRAINING: DOES IT WORK?

One of the most consistent findings in the literature on social skills training is the targeting and training of specific skills does lead to improvements in children's ability to perform these skills. Social skills training programs that combine direct instruction with modeling and coaching of specific skills and prosocial behaviors have been found to impact children's ability to perform specific social behaviors and skills, including conversational skills (e.g., Bierman & Furman, 1984; Chin & Bernard-Opitz, 2000), self-control (Sim *et al.*, 2006), assertiveness (Antshel & Remer, 2003; Blonk *et al.*, 1996; Epp, 2008), theory of mind skills (Ozonoff & Miller, 1995), and play skills (Barry *et al.*, 2003; Harper *et al.*, 2008) over the short-term. These results have been found across children with a range of social difficulties and diagnoses, including autism spectrum disorders, Attention Deficit Hyperactivity Disorder, social anxiety, and learning disorders. A recent study demonstrated that video modeling of prosocial behaviors lead to greater improvements in social skills for 4 to 6-year-old children diagnosed with autism (Kreoger *et al.*, 2007). While children in both groups showed an increase in prosocial behaviors (including initiations, responses and interventions), children who received direct teaching showed greater gains across the time of the intervention.

However, while social skills interventions that include instruction and coaching of specific skills appear to succeed in improving children's ability to perform these skills, most reviews and meta-analyses point out that there have been few studies that have been able to show that these gains will generalize outside of the treatment setting, or have any impact on broader social functioning, including peer relationships, social status or peer acceptance (Beelman *et al.*, 1994; Greco & Morris, 2001). A recent meta-analysis of school-based studies for children with autism spectrum disorders found that across studies that examined maintenance and generalization of effects, the average effect size was moderate and low, respectively (Bellini *et al.*, 2007). In other words, it appears that gains in skills made during the time of the intervention do not consistently generalize to settings outside of the immediate training condition, and the gains that are made are not maintained over the long term.

Consequently, there has been a strong call to demonstrate broader, real-world effects of social skills training programs, as it is hoped that such programs will impact children's relationships, peer status, and general emotional functioning (Gresham, 1997; Maag, 2006; Rao *et al.*, 2008). To this end, Bierman and Furman (1984) examined the effects of coupling individual skills coaching with positive peer interactions for a non-clinical sample of preadolescents (i.e., students who had been identified as low in peer acceptance). Their results indicated that coaching increased skills acquisition, but positive peer involvement was related to increased peer acceptance, as well as children's improved self-perceptions. This result suggests that in order to make immediate changes in children's broader social and emotional functioning, interventions need to target more than skill acquisition. Peer-mediated strategies have been discussed as an intervention to assist children with positive social interactions in more naturalistic contexts (Guevremont & Dumas, 1994). In a recent school-based study, the incorporation of typical peers was related to improvements in play skills, including turn-taking and social initiation, for children with autism (Harper *et al.*, 2008).

Similarly, in an effort to increase generalization and maintenance of gains, more and more programs are incorporating parents into training. For example, Sim and colleagues (2006) utilized both parent sessions and homework involving play dates in their social skills training program with children with a variety of psychiatric diagnoses. They found that a combination of direct instruction, coaching/modeling, and positive reinforcement for prosocial behaviors resulted in a decrease in externalizing behaviors and improvements in children's ability to interact prosocially with peers. Beaumont and Sofronoff (2008) attempted to increase generalization by providing parent training for children diagnosed with Asperger's Disorder. This study's strengths was the relatively large sample size, as well as its wait-listed control group. Children were taught skills using a computer-based game, and parents participated in simultaneous group sessions designed to reinforce the skills children were learning. According to parent report, children in the intervention group made greater gains in social skills compared to the control group, and these gains were maintained at 5 month follow-up. Finally, Spence *et al.*, (2000) compared their cognitive-behavioral model with and without parental involvement, and found greater improvements when parents were involved in the treatment of children with social anxiety. These studies show promising effects of social skills training when a parental component is incorporated into treatment.

However, while gains made via social skills training might not be immediately visible in real-life social settings in terms of observed skills, or peer relationships, participation in social skills training may impact children's perceptions of their social relationships. Barry *et al.* (2003) found that after learning skills and behaviors that include greetings and play, and spending time interacting with typical peers, high functioning children with autism spectrum disorders showed increased ability to demonstrate these skills with peers in the clinic setting. Although parental reports indicated that only certain skills (e.g., greetings) generalized outside of the clinic setting, the children themselves reported increased perceptions of social support by peers. Increased perception of peer support could contribute to increased interactions with peers, and ultimately, improvements in social skills and competence. Thus, there may be a time delay in our ability to see changes in children's social functioning following social skills training. Prospective, follow-up studies will allow for an examination of longer-term effects of social skills training on children's social competence.

To summarize the major points from the current literature, social skills training appears to have small to moderate overall treatment effects with children with a variety of social skills difficulties and psychiatric diagnoses. Positive effects of social skills training have been found on children's ability to perform specific social skills, including conversation skills, theory of mind skills and play skills over the short-term (e.g., Barry *et al.*, 2003; Bierman & Furman, 1984; Chin & Bernard-Opitz, 2000; Ozonoff & Miller, 1995). However, current interventions and/or our studies of these interventions have limited ability to demonstrate that social skills training produces effects on children's social behaviors or relationships outside the treatment setting or after treatment ends. Social skills training programs that involve parents, typical peers, and real world social contexts appear to increase generalization of skills and maintenance of gains made during training (e.g., Spence *et al.*, 2000), and prospective, longitudinal studies are necessary to examine the potential long-term impact on development and well-being.

A SAMPLING OF SOCIAL SKILLS TRAINING PROGRAMS

In this section, we will describe several of the more commonly utilized social skills training programs. We have chosen to highlight in detail four of these programs that are documented and have relevance to our work in a child outpatient clinic. The programs designed by Michelson and colleagues (Michelson *et al.*, 1983) and Elliot and Gresham (1991) were selected because these were among the first applications of social skills training, identifying and targeting specific skills needed for children to function effectively with their peers. Braswell and Bloomquist (1991) are discussed because of their exclusive focus on children with ADHD utilizing a cognitive-behavioral group therapy approach. Finally, Frankel and Myatt (2003) have designed a program to work with a heterogeneous clinic population. Similar to the population we see at our clinic, their program is designed for children with ADHD, as well as autism spectrum disorders.

The earlier models depicted by Michelson *et al.* (1983) and Elliot and Gresham (1991) are school-based models designed to assist children with social skills training in their classrooms or in a small group with a counselor or therapist. In these programs, specific skills are identified and then taught separately in sessions or classes by trainers who have teaching or counseling backgrounds. The interventions in these programs are time limited, and may consist of anywhere from 6 or 8 to 16 weekly sessions. The program designed by Michelson and colleagues (1983) includes skills-based modules. Within each module, leaders are provided with a rationale for the chosen skill, procedures related to the skill, and material to stimulate group discussion and homework. Some of the specific skills taught include prosocial behaviors (e.g., compliments, turn taking), conversation skills, and emotional skills (e.g., empathy). Leaders are encouraged to utilize modeling of skills, and to involve children in role-playing as well. By working in the classroom, this program allows children with social difficulties to have the benefit of learning from their more socially competent peers.

Drawing from the work and theory of Michelson and colleagues (1983), Elliott and Gresham (1991) have developed a social skills training program for use in schools, utilizing a small group format and a social learning model (e.g., Bandura, 1977). Their program is recommended for children who have a variety of difficulties with social behaviors and skills. The focus is on identifying children with social difficulties, and working in a small group setting. Thus, although this program was designed for use in schools, it could be adapted for use in a clinic setting. Small groups of three to six children meet with a group leader up to twice a week for 45 to 60 minute sessions. Elliott and Gresham presented forty-three skill units, with each skill categorized in one of five domains: cooperation, assertion, responsibility, empathy, and self-control. Leaders choose specific skills based on the needs of the children in the group. Techniques utilized include modeling, behavioral rehearsal, coaching, social problem solving, and homework. They also encourage the use of behavioral and learning principles such as response cost, timeout, overcorrection, and differential reinforcement techniques. In contrast to the method of Michelson and colleagues (1983) who had worked within the classroom, this program tailors interventions to the needs of specific children, creating a more clinical atmosphere. Follow-up booster sessions are recommended after completion of the program in order to promote maintenance toward social gains.

Braswell and Bloomquist's (1991) model is noteworthy in that it is one of only a handful of documented group treatment models employing cognitive-behavioral interventions for children with a diagnosis of ADHD with or without a co-morbid conduct disorder. The program has separate child, parent/family, and school components, which can be applied in either a school or clinic setting. We will focus on the outpatient clinic model here because it is more relevant for our clinical work. The intervention occurs over a 14-week period, in sessions lasting 60 to 90 minutes. Children are trained in problem solving and self-instruction skills in a group format, and are helped to apply these skills in the service of interpersonal problem solving, emotion regulation, and improved behavior. Homework is given to promote generalization. New skills are introduced in each session through didactic instruction, and are practiced through modeling and role-play. Relaxation strategies are also utilized. Therapists and children work together to generate goals focusing on improvements in specific skills (e.g., eye contact, expressing feelings, sharing). A behavioral reinforcement system is utilized and children are rewarded with points for practicing skills and demonstrating prosocial behavior.

A recent clinic-based program is the Children's Friendship Training Program at UCLA (Frankel & Myatt, 2003). The children treated in this program have a variety of diagnoses, including ADHD, Oppositional Defiant Disorder, and autism spectrum disorders. This program is designed primarily for school-age children, who participate in weekly one hour sessions for up to eighteen weeks. Groups consist of a maximum of ten children. To increase generalization, parents also attend concurrent groups designed to assist them to work with their children. This program is syllabus-driven and designed to help children to improve both general peer relations and acceptance, as well as develop and maintain dyadic friendships. Group leaders and coaches from behavioral health backgrounds act as consultants. Behavioral strategies, such as positive reinforcement for prosocial behaviors, and ignoring of inappropriate behaviors, are used within the classes. At each class, a skill is introduced and taught, and is then practiced through play in the classroom or in outside play areas, with leaders serving as coaches to reinforce the skills that are taught. Thus, this program is active and action oriented, and provides children with many opportunities to practice skills through real-world activities and interactions (i.e., sports, games and typical peer interactions). To promote generalization and maintenance of gains, homework is assigned, and is expected to be completed by children, with parental participation.

Chapter 6

THE WEILL CORNELL SOCIAL SKILLS TRAINING PROGRAM

OVERVIEW OF OUR PROGRAM

The Social Skills Training Program at Weill Cornell Medical College, New York Presbyterian Hospital, Payne Whitney Westchester, began in 1995 as a short-term, 12 session group program in the Child and Adolescent Outpatient Department. Since then, the program has expanded to include both short and long-term groups. Children are referred to the program with a variety of social difficulties, including experiences of social rejection and isolation; peer victimization (e.g., teasing and bullying); and as discussed earlier, diagnoses typical of an outpatient child psychiatry setting (e.g., ADHD, anxiety disorders, mood disorders, learning disabilities, adjustment disorders and increasingly, autism spectrum disorders, such as Asperger's Disorder and Pervasive Developmental Disorder, Not Otherwise Specified). While the majority of the children in the program are school age (i.e., ages 6 through 12), we also have groups for high school and college age adolescents, and preschool groups are available as well.

GROUP LEADERS

Our program is located in a child and adolescent outpatient psychiatry clinic and is part of a larger academic medical center. Our group leaders come from a variety of clinical disciplines. Program staff includes clinical social workers and psychologists, as well as trainees in psychology, psychiatry, and social work. Staff and trainees who participate in the program do so on a part-time basis, as part of their varying assignments and duties. Most groups are co-led with a senior leader (staff or faculty) paired with a trainee, and in some groups there may be two trainees paired with a senior group leader. Important to the success of the program is the position of a program director (JRH), whose primary role is to direct and to coordinate the program. The functions of the program director include community outreach, intakes and *in vivo* screening, group placement, troubleshooting when problems occur, and training of the group leaders. She also runs a weekly supervision seminar for group leaders, in which any issues or difficulties can be brought in and discussed with the director and other senior clinicians. All of the trainees in the program also receive supervision from the senior leader of their group.

REFERRAL, EVALUATION, AND GROUP PLACEMENT

Children are referred to the program by community health care providers, schools, and parents. Based on our belief in and understanding of the importance of tailoring training interventions to meet the specific needs of the children, we have developed a comprehensive evaluation process for children prior to their entry into our program. Referrals are screened at first by telephone by the program director, and families are mailed a comprehensive developmental questionnaire. We ask parents to complete this questionnaire, which asks for detailed information regarding the child's developmental, social, medical, educational, and psychiatric history, and return it to us. When this questionnaire is returned, parents are contacted to schedule an evaluation. The evaluation is a team effort, which includes the evaluator, who may be a clinical social worker, child psychiatry fellow, or psychology post-doctoral fellow, an attending psychiatrist, and the director of the evaluation service (BLF), a clinical psychologist who both participates in the evaluation and supervises the evaluator. The evaluator meets with the child and parent, and gathers information from collateral sources. In addition, the child participates in a diagnostic play group, which allows the evaluation team to observe social behaviors and interactions with peers (see Gupta *et al.*, 1996). The breadth of our intake and evaluation process assists greatly with decisions regarding treatment planning and group placement.

Following a team meeting to discuss the case, the diagnosis and treatment plan is finalized with the family. If social skills training appears warranted, then the child is screened for participation in a specific group. This may entail setting up a meeting between the child and family and the group leader(s). If no suitable group is currently available, or if it is determined that social skills training would not be appropriate at this time, then a waiting list for an appropriate group is utilized and/or alternative treatments are recommended. A child may be referred for alternative treatment for a variety of reasons, including psychotic symptoms; suicidal or self-injurious behavior or ideation; borderline intellectual functioning or mental retardation; significant disruptive or aggressive behavior; or severe separation anxiety or refusal to attend group. In this latter case, children may not be "group ready" but with individual coaching sessions, may be able to participate in a group at a later date.

Thus, based on the child's age, gender, and developmental level, as well as information gathered during the evaluation, a specific group is identified for a newly evaluated child. The child is then invited to the program as a "guest" and is encouraged to try the group for three sessions. This allows the child and group leaders to determine if the group is a good fit. A three session "trial period" is usually enough to engage the child and to allow the leaders to make a decision regarding the child's appropriateness for an already existing group. It is the philosophy of the program not to force a child to attend if the child strongly objects. In such cases the child may not be "group ready," and other recommendations are made.

An effort is made to balance the groups so that there is a mix of children with varying strengths and weaknesses within each group. This includes having diagnostic diversity, mixing more passive with active children, and having children of varying verbal strengths within the same group. In this way children can learn from the strengths that others bring to the group. For school-age children, most of the groups are single sex, which is in keeping with developmental preferences. Younger children can be placed in co-ed groups, and for adolescents we often offer both single sex and co-ed groups. Groups usually consist of four to seven members, but we also offer dyads or "mini" groups of three children when this is deemed clinically appropriate.

Group cycles run for approximately twelve to fourteen sessions at a time, following the trimesters of the academic year, with a shorter six to eight session cycle for the summer months. To promote stability, predictability and cohesion, the groups are designed to be closed, with a consistent roster of members. Sessions are one hour in length. Parent feedback occurs at the end of each cycle, or more frequently depending upon clinical need. Parents are also consistently involved in the training via verbal and written updates of group activities, goals, and homework, and are given suggestions for ways to practice and reinforce skills outside of group. Children tend to remain in the program for more than one cycle, and some children remain in the program for several years.

THEORETICAL ORIENTATION

The literature on social skills training is robust with discussion of cognitive and behavioral approaches used in group treatment (see Elliott & Gresham, 1991; Michelson, *et al.*, 1983). These methods focus primarily on content, or what to say and do when teaching specific social skills. While we embrace many of these techniques, and will discuss them in more detail here, we believe that there has been a paucity of emphasis on relational and process oriented approaches in social skills training. These methods are equally emphasized in our program and merit attention. Our orientation and emphasis on process comes from several of the major models of group psychotherapy, including interpersonal (Yalom, 1995) and social systems, or group-as-a-whole (Scheidlinger, 1982). We also draw on the theory and literature on children's group psychotherapy (e.g., Hariton *et al.*, 1991; Schamess, 1986; Scheidlinger, 1982). Our model is integrative in that *both* process and content-oriented approaches are utilized, with our emphasis and focus shifting back and forth as the group requires it.

Our focus on the interpersonal process within the group means that we pay attention to the nature of the relationships among the group members. It entails consideration and understanding of how group members are interacting in the here and now. This focus on the here-and-now is addressed on both the individual and group level. In discussing group-relevant psychoanalytic propositions, Scheidlinger (1982, p. 30) emphasized consideration of the following process-oriented variables: the meaning of behavior; the development of social attitudes and the capacity for group ties; group emotional processes; the role of the leader; and the interaction of individual personalities and group factors. While a comprehensive discussion of these factors is beyond the scope of this book (see Smead, 1995), they are integral to our approach to social skills training.

We also emphasize and utilize unstructured play in our groups (Axline, 1974; Hariton *et al.*, 1991). While children may see this playtime as fun, and we may also utilize this time as a reward for prosocial behaviors, we draw on play as an important method of nonverbal communication that enables children to symbolically express their inner world and conflicts. Although the group leaders model the verbalization of feelings and needs, both verbal and nonverbal communication during sessions are worked with in an effort to understand individual group members, as well as themes expressed by the group as-a-whole. When the timing is felt to be beneficial to the child and or group, insights gleaned from the process are shared with the group members.

The group therapists in our program draw upon a range of interventions depending upon the skill or skills that are emphasized in the session, the make-up and developmental level of the group members they are working with, and the stage of the group process (i.e., beginning, middle, or end stage) (Hariton et al., 1991). For example, at the beginning stages of the group, we focus on the development of group cohesion and may utilize activities that foster cohesion. These activities assist children to develop attachments to each other, the leaders and the group. With school-age children, choosing a group name may be the first group activity, aiding in the development of group cohesion. Similarly, working together to decide on group rules and norms is another early-stage activity that acts in the service of group cohesion.

The consistent relationships, structure, and predictability of the groups promote a therapeutic climate whereby interactions can be fostered and evaluated, feedback between children supported, and friendships developed. Relationships among children sometimes occur outside the group and are viewed as learning opportunities where social interactions can be practiced and potential friendships made. Interpersonal conflicts that inevitably develop over time between members, subgroup formations and pairings between members, and scapegoat tendencies that might arise within the groups are viewed as "grist for the mill" to be worked with by the group. Our process-oriented approach means that we view these dynamics as replicating the roles that our group members have taken on in other settings, and we utilize the group to increase children's understanding of their behavior and its impact on others. As children often become stuck in social roles in their school or home settings, we utilize the group as an arena where new behaviors and roles can be tried out and practiced. Thus, the emphasis on process is vital to our work and goes hand in hand with the skills that are taught and practiced in our program. While teaching social skills to our children, we are acutely sensitive of the potential of group therapy for growth beyond skill development.

TRAINING METHODS

With process as a backdrop, our group leaders select from an array of techniques that promote skill acquisition among the group members. We use a combination of behavioral, cognitive-behavioral, and social-cognitive strategies. Group leaders take an active role in the groups, introducing, teaching, and modeling skills and behaviors. Skills to be addressed are based on the specific difficulties of the children in the group. These difficulties are identified in a number of different ways including the comprehensive evaluation, ongoing communication with parents, *in vivo* observations, and personal goals. While we do not have a single recipe or a fixed week by week curriculum, we draw from a range of interventions, depending on the needs of the specific group. In this section, we will discuss the general strategies we employ to promote the development and generalization of skills. For a more comprehensive discussion of these general methods, the reader is referred to Michelson *et al.* (1983), and Merrell and Gimpel (1998), whose volumes on social skills training provide excellent discussions of these methods. We will then present a sample of specific techniques and interventions that we have found effective and clinically useful in addressing emotional, behavioral, and cognitive skills.

Behavioral techniques include those drawn from operant and social learning models. In addition to helping to foster group cohesion, the creation of group rules also acts in the service of behavior management. We find that having rules and norms (often displayed visually during group sessions) helps support an atmosphere in which skill acquisition and enhancement can occur. Children and leaders work together to generate a list of rules that can be modified as the group cycle progresses. Leaders will also discuss with children the process whereby disruptive behavior will be handled (e.g., warning, cool down, time out). In general, response cost (e.g., time out) is utilized only when behavior is aggressive or disruptive to the group process. We more often rely on the use of positive reinforcement to shape and promote desired behaviors, and negative punishment (e.g., ignoring), to decrease the likelihood of undesirable behaviors (i.e., those that are not disruptive or causing harm to any other members).

Positive reinforcement is used throughout our groups to increase children's prosocial behaviors and demonstration of social skills. Many of our groups utilize a reward system where points, tickets or tokens are earned for demonstration of specific behaviors, including children's individual goals, or goals the group has decided to work towards together. Depending on the preference and needs of the specific children, a group reward will be chosen to celebrate the achievement of a goal. We find that the use of positive reinforcement, including techniques such as prompting of desired behaviors and shaping of successive approximations towards desired behaviors, is extremely useful for children in that it fosters feelings of competence and success. In addition, the feeling of being successful inspires hope and encouragement among children who have frequently thought of themselves as "losers" who cannot change. Furthermore, for some children, particularly those who may be anxious or unable to demonstrate their social skills, receiving praise, tokens and other forms of positive reinforcement may provide a much needed impetus to try out their skills.

We also rely heavily on social learning or modeling of desired behaviors. Leaders frequently model skills and behaviors for children in the context of didactic instruction of skills, structured activities, and unstructured, less formal interactions. Children who are more skilled in an area may also act as models for their less-skilled peers. In conjunction with modeling, we employ coaching in the service of teaching and training new behaviors. Leaders may coach children on skills, and also pair children with their more-skilled peers who may then act as peer-coaches. Individual coaching is also utilized when necessary to assist children who may be struggling within the group. This may entail having a child attend an individual "coaching session" with one of the group leaders prior to the group. This serves to help the child anticipate what to expect in the session, practice and rehearse desired behaviors, and reinforce what has been learned before. We can also discuss with the child and family what specific techniques may be helpful in assisting the child to get the most out of the group sessions.

Cognitive, social cognitive, and problem solving techniques are also drawn from and applied when appropriate. Because children in our groups present a range of social information processing difficulties, we design many of our interventions around improving their understanding of social information, including identification of the feelings, motives, and intentions of others, and interpersonal problem solving. Feelings identification in self and others is a frequent goal of our structured and unstructured activities. Group leaders look for opportunities to assist children to expand their understanding of others' feelings, beliefs and intentions. This may be done through discussion of social experiences, through structured activities, or *in vivo* using the group process. For example, when a conflict or misunderstanding occurs within the group, leaders assist children to understand the possible cognitive distortions or misattributions that may be contributing to the conflict. Problem solving techniques are utilized to assist children to gain a better understanding of how to navigate a range of problems, including interpersonal difficulties. By teaching children the steps to effective problem solving, we hope to provide them not only with a general skill set, but increase their confidence that they can handle problems as they arise.

Other cognitive techniques we rely on include monitoring and identification of thoughts, and understanding of how thoughts impact feelings and behaviors. We frequently teach children to utilize self-talk in a variety of situations. For example, self-talk is taught as a skill that children can use to bolster their self-esteem when they are teased, calm down when they are angry, or to develop the thought process needed for problem solving. Relaxation techniques and skills are taught, and practiced in the groups. For example, we utilize "stress" or "fidget" balls to assist children with a variety of difficulties including sensory integration issues, motoric dysregulation, or inattention. We encourage children to think about and share their own ideas about what helps them to relax or calm down when they are upset.

GROUP FORMAT

Each group session lasts one hour. While leaders prepare a skill and activity to promote the chosen skill for that session, the "skill of the week" can also be prompted by the informal narratives that children bring into the session during an activity that we call "News of the Week" (S. Scheidlinger, personal communication). Sessions often begin with News of the Week, which will be described in greater detail in the following section, while children share a snack that one member has brought in for the entire group. Following News of the Week, the leaders will introduce a skill that will be taught and/or practiced during the session. These skills are selected based on children's individual goals, as well as the overall goals of the group. After a skill is introduced, the leaders will model the skill, discuss the reasons why the skill is important, and engage children in a structured activity that will allow them to practice the skill. These activities may include role-playing, storytelling, narrative building, and cooperative play activities (e.g., board games), and serve to reinforce what has been discussed and demonstrated. We rely on positive reinforcement (e.g., praise, tokens, tickets) to promote the use of the skill, as well as other prosocial or pro-friendship behaviors and skills. The final ten minutes of the group is typically used for free play, in which children are allowed to select a play activity and a peer to play with. This activity allows children to practice skills in a more naturalistic manner. Similarly, in order to promote generalization, children may be given a homework assignment to use or practice the skill in a real-world setting such as at home or school (e.g., calling a peer for a play date). They are then asked to report back to the group regarding their homework. Parents are also informed of the skills that are being addressed in the group and asked to reinforce these skills at home as well.

EXAMPLES OF INTERVENTIONS TO TARGET SPECIFIC SOCIAL SKILLS

Although we draw from a range of interventions, depending on the needs and developmental level of the children, we will now present a small sample of the interventions that we have found to be particularly effective in our work. Referring back to Table 1, which outlines the social skills; we focus on in each of the three broad categories of emotional, behavioral, and cognitive functioning, we have chosen two skills (or families of skills) from each of these domains, and an example of an intervention to address each of these skills.

EMOTIONAL SKILLS

Emotion Recognition

We utilize a variety of structured activities to assist children to improve their ability to label feelings in themselves and others, identify triggers of negative and positive feeling states, and develop strategies to regulate emotions. For school-age children, we might use excerpts from Lindsay's (1995) book *Proud of Our Feelings* or Shapiro's (1993) manual, *All Feelings are OK – It's What You Do With Them That Counts*. Lindsay's book was designed to stimulate interaction between children and parents, but we use it to introduce both positive and negative feelings, and to stimulate discussion of feelings among children in the group. Group members can volunteer to read a page about a particular feeling (if there are no volunteers, an infrequent occurrence, a group leader will read the page), and then members are asked to offer examples describing what circumstances/events/thoughts might trigger the feeling. This activity is followed, over the next several weeks, with those such as role playing, discussing possible coping strategies, and/or creating a cartoon about the feeling. For example, members might create a cartoon about what "a kid" might do in response to a strong feeling that would be "helpful" rather than "unhelpful." The creation of parallel cartoons of 3 or 4 frames portraying both the "helpful" and "unhelpful" way of reacting is a particularly powerful technique to generate discussion and provide a safe atmosphere that allows children to discuss the more negative behaviors that they may typically use outside the group. Shapiro's manual is a series of cartoons that pose a question about a wide variety of events. For example, one cartoon shows a child being pointed at by peers and the text under the cartoon asks "How do you react when kids tease you?" Followed by, "What can you do to feel better?" It is possible to use several of the cartoons to generate reactions and coping strategies from members in response to being teased, bullied, or rejected by a peer. Their individual responses can then be used to create a guide for other children.

Self-Esteem

Many of the children present for outpatient social skills training are described by parents as having low self-esteem (and our own data backs up this observation). Their behaviors suggest that their self- appraisals are largely negative and the children themselves often report being victims of teasing, bullying, and peer rejection. A small subset of the children in the group program defend against their negative self-appraisal with a grandiose façade, engaging in exaggerated reports of their social, academic, and athletic abilities. As a result, we focus many of our activities on assisting children to develop positive and realistic feelings and perceptions of themselves. While we believe that being a member of a group serves to provide a child with a sense of belonging and competency, which translates into improved self-esteem, we also utilize a variety of structured interventions to increase positive but realistic self-appraisals. To this end, one activity we have found useful involves having group members create their own advertisements. These advertisements utilize positive and negative characteristics provided by the leaders with additional characteristics generated by the group members themselves. We have members create the advertisements about themselves and each of their parents. These advertisements are created over several sessions and the children are instructed that they must include one negative characteristic for each advertisement. Younger children are encouraged to use both words and drawings. Children who have difficulty including a negative characteristic are reminded that an advertisement for their favorite candy would include a "disclaimer." Children who have difficulty generating a list of positive attributes are given group support, with leaders eliciting from other group members what positive attributes they would suggest be included. In addition, we might ask them to create an advertisement for a friend. Such an ad might read "Wanted: a friend who is kind, funny and likes to play video games, but sometimes cannot wait his turn." This would be the beginning of a discussion, cartoon, or role playing exercise regarding characteristics that might be somewhat negative but can be acceptable in a friend, versus negative characteristics that would eliminate a peer from consideration as a friend. Self-esteem is also enhanced when the individual group members begin to develop a sense of their parents as less than perfect individuals and is a building block for the development of an integrated sense of self.

BEHAVIORAL SKILLS

Communication Skills

The development and/or enhancement of effective communication skills is a significant objective in our group work, as many of the children enrolled in our program struggle with verbal and non-verbal communication. To assist with both verbal and non-verbal communication skills, we utilize an activity that we call "News of the Week." This activity can be tailored for children of different ages, and at different levels of verbal development and skills. We often utilize this activity at the beginning of each group session, thus allowing it to function as an ice-breaker and an opportunity for children to settle into the group. During News of the Week, children are asked to share an event from the past week or an event that will be happening in the upcoming week. Children are encouraged to share any one piece of news; thus, they are given the freedom to share experiences with family, peers, at school or in other areas of their life. Parents are asked to engage in pre-group coaching to aid their children in the preparation of news to share. The primary goal of this activity is to teach, review and reinforce basic communication skills, including eye contact, body language, and use of appropriate rate and volume of speech. In addition, this activity provides direct experience with the give and take of conversation. Members are encouraged to ask each other appropriate follow-up questions pertaining to each other's news. For the children who are listening, this exercise allows them to practice self-control, inhibiting verbally impulsive behaviors and trying not to interrupt their peer. For the child who is sharing, this activity allows him to practice remaining focused and on-topic as he shares his news. Since the children are sharing personal information, this activity also serves an important role in helping members get to know each other, and develop trust and cohesion in the group.

Play and Task Skills

We utilize a number of structured activities to assist children with the development and practice of their cooperative play skills. Skills targeted through these interventions include cooperation and compromise, decision making, turn-taking, conflict resolution, and sharing. The type of activities that we choose may depend on the children's age and developmental level, but generally involves having the children work together on a project. The project can take a variety of forms, including an art project (e.g., a group mural), the telling and writing of a story or some other form of narrative (e.g., a play), or the creation of an imaginary world. Some of the more interesting versions of the latter involve the design and creation of a country (e.g., "Create a Country") or planet, with children working to select such elements as flags, mottos, animals, and mascots. The key element of each of these activities is that children must work together to come to decisions, and all group members must be involved. These activities also allow children to practice on-task behavior. We often use these activities at the beginning of a group cycle as they can also act to promote group cohesion. Some of these activities have been adapted from an excellent workbook on cooperative learning that has been used in classroom settings (Tarpley, 1992).

In addition to communication and play/task behaviors, we target prosocial behaviors, including assertion, self-control, social initiation, following rules and direction, giving and receiving feedback, compromise, cooperation, and flexibility. These are addressed through a combination of structured activities, including board games, as well as unstructured play activities, in which children are given time to work together to select a play activity, and with the support of the leader, to practice these skills. In addition to positive reinforcement, group leaders reward and praise displays of these behaviors as they occur naturally and spontaneously during the group.

COGNITIVE SKILLS

Effort Control

As is frequently observed among children with ADHD and autism spectrum disorders, children in our group program have a variety of deficits and difficulties in the cognitive domain. Many of our activities focus on assisting children to develop more cognitive control over their behavior. To this end, one focus of intervention in the cognitive domain is ignoring, or the skill of inhibiting an impulse to respond to social stimuli. Difficulties ignoring perceived peer provocations or modulating the intensity of responses can often lead to increased peer conflict, inappropriate or disruptive behavior, and further social alienation.

An activity developed by one of the authors (AR) and Josette Banks, Ph.D. to assist with this difficulty is called the "Ignoring Game." This activity assists children to develop and practice self-control and inhibition. In this activity, one group member sits in front of the group while the other members try to make him laugh. Ignoring humor, rather than taunts or ambiguous behavior, was chosen to protect children's feelings, make the game fun, and avoid ethical dilemmas, while practicing the essential cognitive skills of response inhibition and refocusing of attention. When the leader gives the signal, group members begin telling jokes, speaking in funny voices, singing, and being silly in an effort to get the member on the hot seat to laugh. The member on the hot seat must keep his eyes open and cannot cover his ears. The group leader uses a stop watch to time how long each member can sit without responding, and marks each group member's time on a board or score card. Strict rules need to be agreed upon and enforced to prevent members from becoming over-stimulated and inappropriate, or crossing personal boundaries. After each round, leaders engage group members in a discussion with the goals of identifying successful strategies that members used for ignoring and generating other cognitive strategies that could be helpful. Members set personal goals for the length of time they can ignore, and progress is almost always made. Once members start to master the skills, a time limit can be set so everyone can get a turn. Secondary benefits of this activity are that it generates positive affect in the group, builds group cohesion, and highlights the members who are funny but might not otherwise have a chance to demonstrate their sense of humor.

Social Information Processing

As the children in our group program also struggle to process, interpret, and respond appropriately to information in social interactions and situations, we rely on activities that will allow them to develop and practice these skills. One example is called the "Coping Star," developed by one of the authors (BLF) and Heather Robins, Psy.D. This activity helps children learn to generate alternative possibilities for peers' intentions, connect thoughts and feelings to situations, develop coping statements and problem-solving strategies, and appreciate perspectives beyond their own. The activity begins with a brief social situation written inside a star or squiggle shape, with lines coming out of the shape to accommodate written responses. Depending on the age of the children and the size of the group, the activity can be done using colorful markers and a large piece of paper on a table, so that each group member can write around his own part of the star, or with the leader writing on a board that all can see. Some scenarios have included, "Kids are whispering," and "The teacher seems angry." Children are asked to generate a range of possible thoughts and feelings they might have in response to such a situation, to consider options for why the person in the scenario might be doing what they are doing, and to generate coping statements and alternate solutions to these social dilemmas. Children work in their own area on the paper and then share and discuss their responses with the group.

Other activities that can be used to address cognitive skills, especially for younger children include traditional children's games like Simon Says and Red-Light, Green-Light. These games allow children to practice their attention and concentration skills, as well as impulse control. Cognitive flexibility and set-shifting can be taught and practiced by assigning children in dyads to play fast-moving board games. These games also promote prosocial behaviors including compromise and sportsmanship. We ask that the children agree upon the game and the rules. After five or ten minutes of play, all children have to change partners and start the process again. Group discussion can focus on identifying stumbling blocks in this process and generating strategies for negotiating these challenges smoothly.

CONCLUSION

The purpose of this volume was to present current understanding of the importance of children's peer relationships for healthy development, and to discuss and evaluate social skills training, one of the primary clinical tools we have for helping children who have impaired social relationships. We presented data from a real-world outpatient psychiatry clinic that serves children with a range of social difficulties and psychiatric diagnoses. We discussed the nuts and bolts of the social skills training program within this clinic, including an integrative theoretical orientation, and examples of specific interventions that are utilized in clinical work with these children.

While our understanding of the importance of social skills, social competence, and peer relations has increased in the past several decades, greater understanding of the specific social difficulties that we observe in children with different clinical presentations and diagnoses is needed. Diagnostic nomenclature should place greater emphasis on disturbances in peer relationships, as children with a variety of psychiatric disorders struggle in this area. Through greater emphasis on and understanding of children's social difficulties, intervention strategies can be designed more effectively and tailored to match difficulties resulting from skill, knowledge, and performance deficits.

Furthermore, as we design our intervention strategies, we also need to ensure that these strategies can be examined and evaluated empirically. In the current climate of managed care, which brings with it more stringent criteria for payment for services, the need to demonstrate treatment effectiveness is paramount. While clinical observations and research provide evidence of short-term gains resulting from social skills training, more research is needed to support the broader and longer-term effects of social skills training. This research would be greatly assisted by the development and use of more sensitive standardized measures to assess social skills, as well as by studies with larger sample sizes and control or comparison groups. Finally, prospective, longitudinal studies that provide follow-up data are necessary to demonstrate that gains made via social skills training have a long-term impact on children's well-being.

The goals of our social skills training program are to help children learn and demonstrate socially skilled behaviors, gain a better understanding of social situations and interactions, and to feel more comfortable with challenging or unfamiliar social situations. We expect that participation in the social skills program will have a deeper impact on their social and emotional functioning. Calling on the work of Malekoff (1997), we endorse the importance of broader objectives in our group work, including the development of children's sense of social and personal competence and belonging, self-discovery, invention, and creativity. We help parents better understand their child's social world so that they may guide their child through life's complex and often times confusing social challenges.

Clinical interventions for social skills should continue to focus on a combination of teaching specific skills and assisting children to generalize these skills outside of the group setting. This can be done through a combination of parental involvement, peer support, and an integrative clinical focus that takes into account a broad range of emotional, behavioral and cognitive skills. It is only through a combination of solid research, and sound, theoretically grounded clinical work that we can truly assist children who struggle daily in their social interactions to have more satisfying relationships and ultimately, happier, healthier lives.

REFERENCES

Abikoff, H., Hectman, L., Klein, R.G., Gallagher, R., Fleiss, K., Etcovitch, J., Cousins, L., Greenfield, B., Martin, D., & Pollack, S. (2004). Social functioning in children with ADHD treated with long-term methylphenidate and multimodal psychosocial treatment. *J Amer Acad Child & Adolescent Psych, 43*, 820-829.

Achenbach, T.M. (1991). *Manual for the Child Behavior Checklist Profile 4/18*. Burlington: University Associates in Psychiatry.

Achenbach, T.M., & Rescorla, L. (2004). The Achenbach System of Empirically Based Assessment (ASEBA) for ages 1.5 to 18 years. *The Use of Psychological Testing for Treatment Planning and Outcome Assessment: Volume 2: Instruments for Children and Adolescents* (3rd ed.). pp. 179-213. Mahwah, NJ: Lawrence Erlbaum Associates.

American Psychiatric Association (2000). *Diagnostic and Statistical Manual of Mental Disorders* (4th ed., Text Revision). Washington, DC: American Psychiatric Association.

Antshel, K.M., & Remer, R. (2003). Social skills training in children with attention deficit hyperactivity disorder: A randomized-controlled clinical trial. *J Clin Child & Adolescent Psychol, 32*, 153-165.

Attwood, T. (2007). *The Complete Guide to Asperger's Syndrome*. Philadelphia: Jessica Kingsley Publishers.

Axline, V. (1969). *Play Therapy*. New York: Ballentine Books.

Bagwell, C.L., Molina, B.S.G., Pelham, W.E., & Hoza, B. (2001). Attention-Deficit Hyperactivity Disorder and problems in peer relations: Predictions from childhood to adolescence. *J Acad Child & Adolescent Psych, 40*, 1285-1292.

Bagwell, C.L., Newcomb, A.F., & Bukowski, W.M. (1998). Preadolescent friendship and peer rejection as predictors of adult adjustment. *Child Develop, 69*, 140 - 153.

Bandura, A. (1977). *Social Learning Theory*. Englewood Cliffs, NJ: Prentice-Hall.

Barkley, R.A. (1997). Behavioral inhibition, sustained attention, and executive functions: Constructing a unifying theory of ADHD. *Psychol Bulletin, 121*, 65-94.

Barkley, R.A. (2003). Attention-deficit/hyperactivity disorder. In E.J. Mash & R.A. Barkley (Eds.), *Child Psychopathology* (pp. 75-143) (2nd ed.). New York: Guildford Press.

Barkley, R.A., DuPaul, G.J., & McMurray, M.B. (1990). Comprehensive evaluation of attention deficit disorder with and without hyperactivity as defined by research criteria. *J Consulting & Clin Psychol, 58*, 775-789.

Barry, T.D., Klinger, L.G., Lee, J.M., Palardy, N., Gilmore, T., & Bodin, S.D. (2003). Examining the effectiveness of an outpatient clinic-based social skills group for high-functioning children with autism. *J Autism & Develop Disorders, 3*, 685-701.

Beaumont, R., & Sofronoff, K. (2008). A multi-component social skills intervention for children with Asperger's Syndrome: The junior detective training program. *J Child Psychol & Psych, 49*, 743 -753.

Beelman, A., Pfingsten, U., & Losel, F. (1994). Effects of training social competence in children: A meta-analysis of recent evaluation studies. *J Clin Child Psychol, 23*, 260-271.

Beidel, D.C., & Turner, S.M. (1998). *Shy Children, Phobic Adults: Nature andTtreatment of Social Phobia*. Washington, DC: American Psychological Association.

Beidel, D.C., Turner, S.M., & Morris, T.L. (1999). Psychopathology of childhood social phobia. *J Amer Acad Child & Adolescent Psych, 38*, 643-650.

Bellini, S., Peters, J.K., Benner, L., & Hope, A. (2007). A meta-analysis of school-based social skills interventions for children with autism spectrum disorders. *Remedial & Special Ed, 28*, 153-162.

Berndt, T.J. (1982). The features and effects of friendship in early adolescence. *Child Develop, 53*, 1447-1460.

Berndt, T.J., & Burgy, L. (1996). Social self-concept. *Handbook of Self-Concept: Developmental, Social, and Clinical Considerations* (pp. 171-209). Oxford: John Wiley & Sons.

Bernstein, G.A., Bernat, D.H., Davis, A.A., & Layne, A.E. (2008). Symptom presentation and classroom functioning nonclinical sample of children with social phobia. *Depression & Anxiety, 25*, 752-760.

Biederman, J. (2005). Attention-Deficit/Hyperactivity Disorder: A selective overview. *Biol Psych, 57*, 1215-1220.

Bierman, K.L., & Furman, W. (1984). The effects of social skills training and peer involvement on the social adjustment of preadolescence. *Child Develop, 55*, 151-162.

Blonk, R.W., Prins, P.J., Sergeant, J.A., Ringrose, J., & Brinkman, A. (1996). Cognitive-behavioral group therapy for socially incompetent children: Short-term maintenance effects with a clinical sample. *J Clin Child Psychol, 25*, 215-224.

Braswell, L., & Bloomquist, M.L. (1991). *Cognitive Behavioral Therapy with ADHD Children: Child, Family and School Interventions.* New York: Guilford.

Bronfenbrenner, U. (1979). *The Ecology of Human Development.* Cambridge, MA: Harvard University Press.

Buhrmester, D. U. (1996). Need fulfillment, interpersonal competence, and the developmental contexts of early adolescent friendship. In W.M. Bukowski, A.F. Newcomb, and W.W. Hartup (Eds.), *The CompanyThey Keep: Friendship in Childhood and Adolescence* (pp. 158-185). New York: Cambridge University Press.

Buhrmester, D., & Furman, W. (1987). The development of companionship and intimacy. *Child Develop, 58*, 1101-1113.

Buhrmester, D., Whalen, C., Henker, B., & MacDonald, V. (1992). Prosocial behavior in hyperactive boys: Effects of stimulant medication and comparison with normal boys. *J Abnormal Child Psychol, 20*, 103-121.

Bukowski, W.M., Hoza, B., & Boivin, M. (1993). Popularity, friendship, and emotional adjustment during adolescence. In B. Laursen (Ed.), *Close Friendships in Adolescence. New Directions for Child Development, 60.* San Francisco: Jossey-Bass.

Cartwright-Hatton, S., Hodges, L., & Porter, J. (2003). Social anxiety in childhood: The relationship with self and observer rated social skills. *J Child Psychol & Psych, 44*, 737-742.

Cartwright-Hatton, S., Tschernitz, N., & Gomersall, H. (2005). Social anxiety in children: Social skills deficit, or cognitive distortion? *Behav Res & Therapy, 43*, 131-141.

Chin, H.Y., & Bernard-Opitz, V. (2000). Teaching conversation skills to children with autism: Effect on the development of a theory of mind. *J Autism & Develop Disorders, 30*, 569-583.

Cichetti, D. (1996). Developmental theory: Lessons from the study of risk and psychopathology. *Psychopathology: The Evolving Science of Mental Disorder* (pp. 253-284). New York: Cambridge University Press.

Coie, J.D., Lochman, J.E., Terry, R., & Hyman, C. (1992). Predicting early adolescent disorder from childhood aggression and peer rejection. *J Consulting & Clin Psychol, 60*, 783-792.

Coy, K., Speltz, M.L., DeKlyen, M., & Jones, K. (2001). Social-cognitive processes in preschool boys with and without oppositional defiant disorder. *J Abnormal Child Psychol, 29*, 107-119.

Crick, N.R., & Dodge, K.A., (1996). Social information processing mechanisms in reactive and proactive aggression. *Child Develop, 67*, 993-1002.

Criss, M.M., Pettit, G.S., Bates, J.E., Dodge, K.E., & Lapp, A.L. (2002). Family adversity, positive peer relationships, and children's externalizing behavior: A longitudinal perspective on risk and resilience. *Child Develop, 73*, 1220-1237.

Diamantopoulou, S., Henricsson, L., & Rydell, A.M. (2005). ADHD symptoms and peer relations of children in a community sample: Examining associated problems, self-perceptions, and gender differences. *Intl J Behav Develop, 29*, 388-398.

Dodge, K.A. (1983). Behavioral antecedents of peer social status. *Child Develop, 54*, 1386-1399.

Dodge, K.A., Bates, J.E., & Pettit, G.S. (1990). Mechanisms in the cycle of violence. *Sci, 250*, 1678 - 1683.

Dodge, K.A., Lansford, J.E., Burks, V.S., Bates, J.E., Pettit, G.S., Fontaine, R., & Price, J.M. (2003). Peer rejection and social-information processing factors in the development of aggressive behavior problems in children. *Child Develop, 74*, 374-393.

Eisenberg, N., Fabes, R., Nyman, M., Bernzweig, J., & Pinuelas, A. (1994). The relations of emotionality and regulation to children's anger-related reactions. *Child Develop, 65*, 109-128.

Elliott, S.N., & Gresham, F.E. (1987). Children's social skills: Assessment and classification practices. *J Counseling & Develop, 66*, 96-99.

Elliott, S.N., & Gresham, F.E. (1991). *Social Skills Intervention Guide: Practical Strategies for Social Skills Training*. Circle Pines, MN: American Guidance Service, Inc.

Epp, K.M. (2008). Outcome-based evaluation of a social skills program using art therapy and group therapy for children on the autistic spectrum. *Children & Schools, 30*, 27-36.

Erath, S., Flanagan, K.S., & Bierman, K.L. (2007). Social anxiety and peer relations in early adolescence: Behavioral and cognitive factors. *J Abnormal Child Psychol, 35*, 405-416.

Erdley, C.A., Nangle, D.W., Newman, J.E., & Carpenter, E.M. (2001). Childrens' friendship experiences and psychological adjustment: Theory and research. In D.W. Nangle & C.A. Erdley (Eds.), *The Role of Friendship in Psychological Adjustment. New Directions for Child Development, 91*. San Francisco: Jossey Bass.

Erhardt, D., & Hinshaw, S.P. (1994). Initial sociometric impressions of attention-deficit hyperactivity disorder and comparison boys: Predictions from social behavior and from nonbehavioral variables. *J Consulting & Clin Psychol, 62*, 833-842.

Frankel, F., & Feinberg, D. (2002). Social problems associated with ADHD vs. ODD in children referred for friendship problems. *Child Psych & Human Develop, 33*, 125-146.

Frankel, F., & Myatt, R. (1996). Self-esteem, social competence and psychopathology in boys without friends. *Personality & Individual Differences, 20*, 401-407.

Frankel, F., & Myatt, R. (2003). *Children's Friendship Training*. New York: Brunner-Routledge.

Greco, L.A., & Morris, T.L. (2001). Treating childhood shyness and related behavior: Empirically evaluated approaches to promote positive social interactions. *Clin Child & Family Psychol Rev, 4*, 299-318.

Greco, L.A., & Morris, T.L. (2005). Factors influencing the link between social anxiety and peer acceptance: Contributions of social skills and close friendships during middle childhood. *Behav Therapy, 36*, 197-205.

Greene, R.W., Biederman, J., Faraone, S.V., Wilens, T.E., Mick, E., & Blier, H.K. (1999). Further validation of social impairment as a predictor of substance use disorders: Findings from a sample of siblings of boys with and without ADHD. *J Clin Child Psychol, 28*, 349-354.

Greene, M.L., & Way. N. (2005). A growth curve analysis of self-esteem among urban, ethnic minority adolescents: Exploring patterns and predictors of change. *J Res Adolescence, 15*, 151-178.

Gresham, F.M. (1986). Conceptual and definitional issues in the assessment of children's social skills: Implications for classification and training. *J Clin Child Psychol, 15*, 3-15.

Gresham, F.M. (1997). Social competence and students with behavior disorders: Where we've been, where we are, and where we should go. *Ed & Treat Children, 20*, 233-249.

Gresham, F.M., & Elliott, S.N. (1990). *The Social Skills Rating System*. Circle Pines, MN: American Guidance.

Gresham, F.M., MacMillan, D.L., Bocian, K.M., Ward, S.L., & Forness, S.R. (1998). Comorbidity of hyperactivity-impulsivity-inattention and conduct problems: Risk factors in social, affective and academic domains. *J Abnormal Child Psychol, 26*, 393-406.

Guevermont, D. (1990). Social skills and peer relationship training. In R. A. Barkley (Ed.), *Attention-Deficit Hyperactivity Disorder: A Handbook for Diagnosis and Treatment* (pp. 540-572). New York: Guilford.

Guevremont, D., & Dumas, M.C. (1994). Peer relationship problems and disruptive behavior disorders. *J Emotional & Behav Disorders, 2*, 164-172.

Gunter, H., Ghaziuddin, M., & Ellis, H. (2002). Asperger syndrome: Tests of right hemisphere functioning and interhemispheric communication. *J Autism & Develop Disorders, 32*, 263-281.

Gupta, M.R., Hariton, J.R., & Kernberg, P.F. (1996). Diagnostic groups for school-age children: Group behavior and DSM-IV diagnosis. In P. Kymissis & D.A. Halperin, (Eds.), *Group Therapy with Children and Adolescents* (pp. 79-96). Washington, DC: American Psychiatric Press.

Hariton, J.R., Kernberg, P.F., & Chazen, S.E. (1991). Play group psychotherapy. In P.F. Kernberg & S.E. Chazen (Eds.), *Children with Conduct Disorders: A Psychotherapy Manual* (pp. 179-285). New York: Basic Books.

Harper, C.B., Symon, J.B.G., & Frea, W.D. (2008). Recess is time-in: Using peers to improve social skills of children with autism. *J Autism & Develop Disorders, 38,* 815-826.

Harter (1985). *The Self-Perception Profile for Children*. Unpublished manual, University of Denver, Denver, CO.

Harter, S. (1999). *The Construction of the Self*. New York: Guilford.

Hartup, W.W. (1996). The company they keep: Friendships and their developmental significance. *Child Develop, 67*, 1-13.

Heiman, T. (2005). An examination of peer relationships of children with and without attention deficit hyperactivity disorder. *School Psychol Intl, 26*, 330-339.

Hinshaw, S.A. (1987). On the distinction between attentional deficits/hyperactivity and conduct problems/aggression in child psychopathology. *Psychol Bulletin, 101*, 443-463.

Hinshaw, S.A. (1994*). Attention Deficits and Hyperactivity in Children.* Thousand Oaks, CA: Sage.

Hinshaw, S.P., & Melnick, S. (1995). Peer relationships in boys with Attention Deficit Hyperactivity Disorder with and without comorbid aggression. *Develop & Psychopathol, 7*, 627-647.

Hoag, M.J., & Burlingame, G.M. (1997). Evaluating the effectiveness of child and adolescent group treatment: A meta-analytic review. *J Clin Child Psychol, 26*, 234-246.

Hoglund, W.L.G., Lalonde, C.E., & Leadbeater, B.J. (2008). Social-cognitive competence, peer rejection and neglect, and behavioral and emotional problems in middle childhood. *Soc Develop, 17*, 528-553.

Hops, H., & Finch, M. (1985). Social competence and skills: A reassessment. In B.H. Schneider, K.H. Rubin & J.E. Ledingham (Eds.), *Children's Peer Relations: Issues in Assessment and Intervention* (pp. 23-39). New York: Springer-Verlag.

Hoza, B., Gerdes, A.C., Hinshaw, S.P., Arnold, L.E., Pelham, W.E., Molina, B.S.G., Abikoff, H.B., Epstein, J.N., Greenhill, L.L., Hectman, L., Adbert, C., Swanson, J.M., & Wigal, T. (2004). Self-perceptions of competence in children with ADHD and comparison children. *J Consulting & Clin Psychol, 72*, 382-391.

Hoza, B., Mrug, S., Gerdes, A.C., Hinshaw, S., Bukowski, W.M., Gold, J.A., Kraemer, H.C., Pelham, W.E., Wigal, T., & Arnold, L.E. (2005). What aspects of peer relationships are impaired in children with Attention-Deficit/Hyperactivity Disorder? *J Consulting & Clin Psychol, 73*, 411-423.

Hoza, B., Pelham, W.E., Dobbs, J., Owns, J.S., & Pillow, D.R. (2002). Do boys with attention deficit hyperactivity disorder have positive illusory self-concepts? *J Abnormal Psychol, 111*, 268-278.

Jensen, P.S., Hinshaw, S.T., Kraemer, H.C., Lenora, N., Newcorn, J.H., Abikoff, H.B., *et al.* (2001). ADHD comorbidity findings from the MTA study: Comparing comorbid subgroups. *J Amer Acad Child & Adolescent Psych, 40*, 147-158.

Kasari, C., & Rotheram-Fuller, E. (2007). Peer relationships of children with autism: Challenges and interventions. In E. Hollander & E. Anagnostou (Eds.), *Clinical Manual for the Treatment of Autism* (pp. 235-257). Washington, DC: American Psychiatric Publishing, Inc.

Katz-Gold, I., Besser, A., & Priel, B. (2007). The role of simple emotion recognition skills among school aged boys at risk of ADHD. *J Abnormal Child Psychol, 35*, 363-378.

Katz-Gold, I., & Priel, B. (2009). Emotion, understanding, and social skills among boys at risk of attention deficit hyperactivity disorder. *Psychol Schools, 46*, 658-678.

Keefe, K., & Berndt, T. (1996). Relations of friendship quality to self-esteem in early adolescence. *J Early Adolescence, 16*, 110-129.

Kernberg, P.F., Clarkin, A.J., Greenblatt, E., & Cohen. J. (1992). The Cornell Interview of Peers and Friends: Development and validation. *J Amer Acad Child & Adolescent Psych, 31*, 483-489.

Kroeger, K.A., Schultz, J.R., & Newsome C. (2007). A comparison of two group-delivered social skills programs for young children with autism. *J Autism & Develop Disorders, 37*, 808-817.

Kupersmidt, J.B., & Coie, J.D. (1990). Preadolescent peer status, aggression, and school adjustment as predictors of externalizing problems in adolescence. *Child Develop, 61*, 1350-1362.

Kupersmidt, J., & Dodge, K. (2004). *Children's Peer Relations: From Development to Intervention.* Washington, DC: American Psychological Association.

Ladd, G.W. (1999). Peer relationships and social competence during early and middle childhood. *Ann Rev Psychol, 50*, 333-359.

Ladd, G.W., & Troop-Gordon, W. (2003). The role of chronic peer difficulties in the development of children's psychological adjustment problems. *Child Develop, 74*, 1344-1367.

Landau, S., & Milich, R. (1988). Social communication patterns of attention-deficit disordered boys. *J Abnormal Psychol, 16*, 69-81.

Landau, S., & Moore, L.A. (1991). Social skills deficits in children with ADHD. *School Psychol Rev, 20*, 235-251.

La Greca, A.M., & Lopez, N. (1998). Social anxiety among adolescents: Linkages with peer relations and friendships. *J Abnormal Child Psychol, 26*, 83-94.

Lindsey, L. (1995). *Proud of Our Feelings.* Washington, DC: Magination Press.

Maag, J.W. (2006). Social skills training for students with emotional and behavioral disorders: A review of reviews. *Behav Disorders, 32*, 5-17.

Macintosh, K., & Dissanayake, C. (2006). Social skills and problem behaviors in school aged children with high-functioning Autism and Asperger's disorder. *J Autism & Develop Disorders, 36*, 1065-1076.

Maedgen, J.W., & Carlson, C.L. (2000). Social functioning and emotional regulation in the attention deficit hyperactivity disorder subtypes. *J Clin Child Psychol, 29*, 30-42.

Malekoff, A. (1997). *Group Work with Adolescents: Principles and Practice.* New York: Guilford.

Malik, N., & Furman, W. (1993). Problems in children's peer relations: What can the clinician do? *J Child Psychol & Psych, 34*, 1303-1326.

McFall, R.M. (1982). A review and reformulation of the concept of social skills. *Behav Assess, 4*, 1-33

Melnick, S.M., & Hinshaw, S.P. (1996). What they want and what they get: The social goals of boys with ADHD and comparison boys. *J Abnormal Child Psychol, 24*, 169-185.

Melnick, S.M, & Hinshaw, S.P. (2000). Emotion regulation and parenting in AD/HD and comparison boys: Linkages with social behaviors and preference. *J Abnormal Child Psychol, 28*, 73-86.

Merrell, K.W., & Gimpel, G.A. (1998). *Social Skills of Children and Adolescents: Conceptualization, Assessment, and Treatment.* Mahwah, NJ: Lawrence Erlbaum Associates.

Michelson, L., & Mannarino, A. (1986). Social skills training with children: Research and clinical applications. In P.S. Strain, M.J. Guralnick, & H.M. Walker (Eds.), *Children's Social Behavior* (pp. 373-407). Orlando: Academic Press.

Michelson, L., Sugai, D.P., Wood, R.P., & Kazdin, A.E. (1983). *Social Skills Assessment and Training with Children. An Empirically Based Handbook.* New York: Plenum Press.

Milich, R., & Dodge, K. (1984). Social information process in child psychiatry populations. *J Abnormal Child Psychol, 12*, 471-489.

Morgan, J., & Banerjee, R. (2006). Social anxiety and self-evaluation of social performance in a nonclinical sample of children. *J Clin Child & Adolescent Psychol, 35*, 292-301.

Murray, D.S., Ruble, L.A., Willis, H., & Molloy, C.A. (2009). Parent and teacher report of social skills in children with autism spectrum disorders. *Lang, Speech, & Hearing Services in Schools, 40*, 109-115.

Myles, B.S., & Southwick, J. (1999). *Asperger Syndrome and Difficult Moments.* Kansas: Autism Asperger Publishing Company.

Newcomb, A.F., & Bagwell, C.L. (1995). Childrens' friendship relations: A meta-analytic review. *Psychol Bulletin, 117*, 306-347.

Newcomb, A., & Bagwell, C.L. (1996). The developmental significance of children's friendship relations. In W. Bukowski, A. Newcomb & W.

Hartup (Eds.), *The Company They Keep: Friendship in Childhood and Adolescence* (pp. 289-321). New York: Cambridge University Press.

Nijmeijer, J.S., Minderaa, R.B., Buitelaar, J.K., Mulligan, A., Hartman, C.A., & Hoekstra, P.J. (2008). Attention-deficit/hyperactivity disorder and social dysfunction. *Clin Psychol Rev, 28*, 692-708.

Ollendick, T., Weist, M., Borden, M., & Greene, R. (1992). Sociometric status and academic, behavioral, and psychological adjustment: A five-year longitudinal study. *J Consulting & Clin Psychol, 60*, 80-87.

Ozonoff, S., & Miller, J.N. (1995). Teaching theory of mind: A new approach to social skills training for individuals with autism. *J Autism & Develop Disorders, 25*, 415-433.

Parker, J.G., & Asher, S.R. (1987). Peer relations and later personal adjustment. Are low-accepted children at risk? *Psychol Bulletin, 102*, 357-389.

Piaget, J. (1932/1965). *The Moral Judgment of the Child.* New York: Free Press.

Pope, A.W., Bierman, K.L., & Mumma, G.H. (1991). Behavior dimensions associated with peer rejection in elementary school boys. *Develop & Psychopathol, 27*, 663-671.

Powers, M., & Poland, J. (2003). *Asperger Syndrome and Your Child. A Parent's Guide.* New York: Harper Collins.

Quiggle, N.L., Garber, J., Panak, W.F., & Dodge, K.A. (1992). Social information processing in aggressive and depressed children. *Child Develop, 63*, 1305-1320.

Quinn, M.M., Kavale, K.A., Mathur, S.R., Rutherford, R.B., & Forness, S.R. (1999). A meta-analysis of social skill interventions for students with emotional or behavioral disorders. *J Emotional & Behav Disorders, 7*, 54-64.

Rao, P.A., Beidel, D.C., & Murray, M.J. (2008). Social skills interventions for children with Asperger's syndrome or high functioning autism: A review and recommendations. *J Autism & Develop Disorders, 38*, 353-361.

Rao, P.A., Beidel, D.C., Turner, S.M., Ammerman, R.T., Crosby, L.E., & Sallee, F.R. (2007). Social anxiety disorder in childhood and adolescence: Descriptive psychopathology. *Behav Res & Therapy, 45,* 1181-1191.

Raudenbush, S.W., & Bryk, A.S. (2002). *Hierarchical Linear Models* (2nd Edition). Thousand Oaks, CA: Sage.

Rogosa, D.R., & Willett, J.B. (1985). Understanding correlates of change by modeling individual differences in growth. *Psychometrika, 50*, 203-228.

Rourke, B.P. (1989). *Nonverbal Learning Disabilities: The Syndrome and the Model*. New York: Guilford Press.

Rourke, B.P. (1995). *Syndrome of Nonverbal Learning Disabilities: Neurodevelopmental Manifestations*. New York: Guilford Press.

Rubin, K., Chen, X., McDougall, P., Bowker, A., & McKinnon, J. (1995). The Waterloo Longitudinal Project: Predicting internalizing and externalizing problems in adolescence. *Develop & Psychopathol, 7*, 751-764.

Rubin, K. & Burgess, K. (2001). Social withdrawal and anxiety. *The Developmental Psychopathology of Anxiety* (pp. 407-434). New York: Oxford University Press.

Schamess, G. (1986). Differential diagnosis and group structure in the outpatient treatment of latency age children. In A.E. Reister, & I.A.Kraft, *Child Group Psychotherapy: Future Tense* (pp. 29-68). Madison, WI: International Universities Press, Inc.

Scheidlinger, S. (personal communication) - cited on p. 42

Scheidlinger, S. (1982). *Focus on Group Psychotherapy: Clinical Essays*. New York: International Universities Press.

Schneider, B.H. (1992). Didactic methods for enhancing children's peer relations: A quantitative review. *Clin Psychol Rev, 12*, 363-382.

Schenider, B.H., & Byrne, B.M. (1985). Children's social skills training: A meta-analysis. In B.H. Schneider, K.H. Rubin, & J.E. Ledingham (Eds.), *Children's Peer Relations: Issues in Assessment and Intervention* (pp. 175-192). New York: Springer.

Selman, R.L. (1980). *The Growth of Interpersonal Understanding*. New York: Academic Press.

Shapiro, L.E. (1993). *All Feelings are OK: It's What You Do With Them That Counts*. King of Prussia, PA: The Center for Applied Psychology, Inc.

Sim, L., Whiteside, S.P., Dittner, C.A., & Mellon, M. (2006). Effectiveness of a social skills training program with school age children: Transition to the clinical setting. *J Child & Family Studies, 15*, 409-418.

Simonian, S.J., Beidel, D.C., Turner, S.M., Berkes, J.L., & Long, J.H. (2001). Recognition of facial affect by children and adolescents diagnosed with social phobia. *Child Psych & Human Develop, 32*, 137-145.

Smead, R. (1995). *Skills and Techniques for Group Work with Children and Adolescents*. Champaign, IL: Research Press.

Smollar, J., & Youniss, J. (1982). Social development through friendship. In K.H. Rubin, & H.S. Ross (Eds.), *Peer Relationships and Social Skills in Childhood*. New York: Springer-Verlag.

Spence, S.H. (1995). *Social Skills Training: Enhancing Social Competence in Children and Adolescents*. Windsor, UK. The NFER-Nelson Publishing Company.

Spence, S.H. (2003). Social skills training with children and young people: Theory, evidence and practice. *Child & Adolescent Mental Hlth, 8*, 84-96.

Spence, S.H., Donovan, C., & Brechman-Toussaint, M. (1999). Social skills, social outcomes, and cognitive features of childhood social phobia. *J Abnormal Psychol, 108*, 211-221.

Spence, S.H., Donovan, C., & Brechman-Toussaint, M. (2000). The treatment of childhood social phobia: The effectiveness of a social skills training-based, cognitive-behavioral intervention, with and without parental involvement. *J Child Psychol & Psych, 41*, 713-726.

Spencer, T.J. (2006). ADHD and comorbidity in childhood. *J Clin Psych, 67*, 27-31.

Sullivan, H.S. (1953). *The Interpersonal Theory of Psychiatry*. New York: WW Norton.

Tarpley, B. (1992). *Cooperative Learning*. Greensboro, NC: Carson-Dellosa Publishing Company.

Thompson, S. (1997). *The Source for Nonverbal Learning Disorders*. Illinois: LinguiSystems, Inc.

Thorell, L.B., & Rydell, A.M. (2008). Behavior problems and social competence deficits associated with symptoms of attention-deficit/hyperactivity disorder: Effects of age and gender. *Child: Care, Hlth & Develop, 34*, 584-595.

Thurber, J.R., Heller, T.L., & Hinshaw, S.P. (2002). The social behaviors and peer expectations of girls with attention deficit hyperactivity disorder and comparison girls. *J Clin Child & Adolescent Psychol, 31*, 443-452.

Vernberg, E.M. (1990). Psychological adjustment and experiences with peers during early adolescence: Reciprocal, incidental, or unidirectional relationships? *J Abnormal Child Psychol, 18*, 187-198.

Volkmar, F., & Klin, A. (1998). Asperger syndrome and nonverbal learning disabilities. In E. Schopler, G. Mesibov, & L. Kunce (Eds.), *Asperger Syndrome or High Functioning Autism?* (pp. 107-121). New York: Plenum Press.

Wheeler, J., & Carlson, C. (1994). The social functioning of children with ADD with hyperactivity and ADD without hyperactivity: A comparison of their peer relations and social deficits. *J Emotional & Behav Disorders, 2*, 2-12.

Willet, □., and Singer, □., (2004) – cited on p. 4

Woodward, L.J., & Fergusson, D.M. (1999). Childhood peer relationship problems and psychosocial adjustment in late adolescence. *J Abnormal Child Psychol, 27*, 87-104.

Yalom, I. (1995). *The Theory and Practice of Group Psychotherapy* (4th ed.). New York: Basic Books.

INDEX

M

maintenance, 29, 30, 32, 33, 53
management, 8, 22, 40
measures, 17, 50
medication, 22, 53
memory, 12
mental disorder, 51, 54
mental health, 20
mental retardation, 37
meta-analysis, 29, 52, 60, 61
methylphenidate, 51
model, 3, 6, 7, 30, 32, 38, 39, 41, 42, 61
modeling, 3, 6, 27, 28, 29, 31, 32, 40, 41, 61
models, 3, 31, 32, 38, 40, 41
mood, 14, 22, 25, 35
mood disorder, 22, 35
mood swings, 14
moral development, 1
moral judgment, 60
motives, 8, 41
motor skills, 6

N

narratives, 42
negative consequences, 18
negative emotions, 15
negative experiences, 2
neglect, 13, 57
non-clinical population, 20, 28

O

objectives, 50
observations, 13, 40, 49
operant conditioning, 27
Oppositional Defiant Disorder, 33
order, 16, 20, 21, 22, 29, 32, 43
orientation, 38, 49

P

parental involvement, 30, 50, 62
parental participation, 33
parenting, 59
parents, 6, 9, 11, 17, 19, 20, 21, 22, 25, 29, 30, 33, 36, 40, 43, 44, 50
passive, 37
peer conflict, 47
peer group, 1, 5
peer rejection, 2, 3, 4, 13, 15, 17, 44, 52, 54, 57, 60
peer relationship, vii, 2, 3, 4, 9, 13, 16, 18, 19, 20, 22, 25, 27, 29, 30, 49, 54, 56, 57, 63
peer support, 30, 50
peers, 1, 2, 3, 4, 6, 10, 11, 12, 13, 14, 15, 16, 17, 18, 19, 20, 22, 25, 29, 30, 31, 36, 41, 44, 45, 48, 56, 63
perceptions, 16, 18, 20, 22, 25, 30, 44, 57
personal communication, 42
personal goals, 40, 47
personality, 1
planning, 7, 12, 18, 36, 51
play activity, 42, 46
Poland, 11, 60
poor, 1, 3, 9, 12, 14, 15, 17, 27
population, 13, 21, 25, 31
positive reinforcement, 29, 33, 40, 41, 42, 46
preadolescents, 3, 29
predictability, 37, 39
predictors, 2, 52, 56, 58
preference, 15, 41, 59
preschool, 35, 54
primary school, 11
problem behavior, 20, 59
problem behaviors, 20, 59
problem solving, 6, 8, 11, 14, 32, 41, 42
problem-solving, 12, 48
problem-solving strategies, 48
program, vii, 19, 21, 22, 25, 28, 29, 31, 32, 35, 36, 37, 38, 39, 44, 45, 47, 48, 49, 50, 52, 55, 62

prosocial behavior, 8, 15, 17, 28, 29, 31, 32, 33, 38, 40, 46, 48
psychiatric diagnosis, 22
psychiatric disorders, 19, 49
psychiatrist, 36
psychology, 36
psychometric properties, 20, 21
psychopathology, 52, 54, 55, 57, 61
psychotherapy, 22, 38, 56, 61, 63
psychotic symptoms, 37
punishment, 5, 40

R

range, 2, 27, 28, 39, 40, 41, 43, 48, 49, 50
reading, 8, 12
recognition, 8, 58
regulation, 10, 13, 54, 59
reinforcement, 5, 32, 40
rejection, 2, 3, 5, 13, 15, 17, 35, 54
relationship, 3, 6, 53, 56
right hemisphere, 56
risk, 3, 4, 15, 54, 58, 60
role playing, 44, 45
role-playing, 31, 42

S

school, vii, 2, 6, 9, 27, 28, 29, 31, 32, 33, 35, 36, 37, 39, 43, 45, 52, 53, 56, 58, 59, 62
school adjustment, 58
scores, 20, 21, 22, 23
searching, 5
self-concept, 53, 57
self-confidence, 11
self-control, 7, 8, 11, 20, 28, 32, 46, 47
self-discovery, 50
self-esteem, 1, 2, 3, 4, 8, 11, 21, 22, 25, 42, 44, 56, 58
self-perceptions, 15, 29, 54
separation, 37
sex, 1, 37
sharing, 32, 46

skill acquisition, 29, 40
skills, vii, 1, 4, 5, 6, 7, 10, 11, 12, 13, 16, 17, 18, 19, 20, 22, 25, 27, 28, 29, 30, 31, 32, 33, 37, 38, 39, 40, 41, 42, 43, 45, 46, 47, 48, 49, 50, 51, 54, 55, 56, 57, 58, 59, 61, 62
skills training, vii, 19, 22, 25, 27, 28, 30, 31, 37, 38, 49, 51, 59, 62
social acceptance, 21
social activities, 9
social adjustment, 53
social anxiety, 11, 17, 18, 28, 30, 55
social attitudes, 38
social behavior, 7, 8, 11, 14, 15, 16, 17, 18, 28, 30, 32, 36, 55, 59, 63
social cognition, 15
social competence, vii, 4, 6, 7, 9, 10, 18, 20, 27, 30, 49, 52, 55, 58, 62
social context, 30
social dilemma, 48
social impairment, 55
social information processing, 8, 41
social learning, 7, 32, 40, 41
social learning theory, 7
social phobia, 52, 53, 62
social problems, 17
social relations, 1, 4, 15, 30, 49
social relationships, 1, 4, 15, 30, 49
social roles, 39
social rules, 11
social situations, 7, 15, 17, 18, 50
social skills, vii, 1, 4, 5, 6, 7, 9, 10, 13, 16, 17, 19, 20, 21, 22, 23, 25, 27, 28, 29, 30, 31, 37, 38, 39, 40, 43, 44, 49, 50, 52, 53, 55, 56, 58, 59, 60, 61, 62
social skills training, vii, 10, 19, 21, 22, 23, 25, 27, 28, 29, 30, 31, 37, 38, 40, 44, 49, 50, 53, 55, 60, 61, 62
social status, 14, 29, 54
social support, 30
social withdrawal, 14, 17
social workers, 36
special education, 20
spectrum, vii, 7, 9, 10, 11, 12, 13, 22, 25, 28, 29, 30, 31, 33, 35, 47, 52, 55, 60